Fifth Edition

THE Work Book

Getting the Job You Want

J. Michael Farr
Richard Gaither
R. Michael Pickrell

Paul Plawin, Consultant
American Vocational Association

 **Glencoe McGraw-Hill**

New York, New York   Columbus, Ohio   Woodland Hills, California   Peoria, Illinois

Inside photography by Dana C. White/Dana White Productions, Inc.

Glencoe/McGraw-Hill

A Division of The McGraw-Hill Companies

Printed in the United States of America.

Send all inquiries to:
Glencoe/McGraw-Hill
21600 Oxnard Street, Suite 500
Woodland Hills, CA 91367

ISBN 0-02-668451-9 (Student Text)
ISBN 0-02-668452-7 (Instructor's Guide)

10 11 12 13 14   024   04 03 02 01 00

·······

CONTENTS

INTRODUCTION

·······

Welcome to the Chase

You've probably heard—it's a tough job market out there. Or perhaps you know from personal experience. Perhaps you're one of the more than 20-plus million people in the United States who will look for a job this year.

What's tough about the job market these days is *change*. Jobs are changing and so are employers, and workers must change with them. Well-paid manufacturing and middle management jobs are disappearing—and not likely to return. The best job possibilities now are with small companies that can change (there's that word again) quickly to meet market conditions. The workers in these companies must be multiskilled and more adaptable (change again). They must be prepared not only to shift jobs within a company but also to shift from company to company as need requires. It is unlikely that they will remain with one or even two employers for their entire careers. Far from it. To stay employed and become well paid, they will have to be as good at changing jobs as they are at doing them.

But *are* most U.S. workers this skilled and adaptable? Well, if you put it that way, maybe they'd hesitate to answer. But if you asked them just whether they needed training in how to look for a job, they'd probably deny it. "I already know how to look for a job," they'd say. "I've been looking—a lot, for months. There just aren't any jobs out there." And all three of those statements would reveal that they know far less than they think they do.

Why Most People Remain Unemployed

One of the biggest barriers to a rewarding job search is the belief in labor-market myths. A few of the most common are listed in the table on the following page.

Myth	Fact
There are no jobs.	This is a "cop-out." More and more small businesses are being started every year. Even in an economy where job growth has slowed, more and more people are working every year.
Hard work, good education, and loyalty guarantee steady work.	Talk with hard-working, loyal, college graduates who are out of work, often after years of steady employment. In today's increasingly competitive global marketplace, there is only one guarantee for steady employment—knowing how to find a job.
All hiring begins at the personnel department.	This is true only for the untrained job seeker. Most job openings are filled before they are even listed. And many businesses don't even have personnel departments.
Most jobs are in *big* companies.	Definitely not true—80 percent of all work is done in small businesses, and 90 percent of all "first hires" occur in such firms.
Employers won't talk to you unless they have an opening.	Wrong—employers are always on the lookout for good workers.
Employers consider only paid work experience.	Employers look for good attitude, education, and a desire to learn—even without experience.
Most interviewers are well trained.	Less than 5 percent of interviewers have professional training. This means that in an interview you might have to assume the roles of both interviewer and interviewee in order to present yourself in the best light.
Interviewers use only logic and reason.	Many interviewers rely on "gut reactions." Since most applicants can't present their skills and don't know what employers want, interviewers have little choice.
Sending out 1,000 resumes gets a job.	One good personal contact is worth 1,000 resumes.
There are good times and bad times to look for work.	Don't be trapped by this thought. While you are looking for work, *all* the time is a good time for job hunting.

Destructive Effects of Extended Unemployment

The average length of unemployment is 3–4 months. Why does it take people so long to find work? Experience shows that people suffer from extended unemployment for three reasons:

1. They don't engage in enough job-search activity.
2. They can't communicate effectively.
3. They make a poor impression based on appearance or behavior.

Notice that all three of these conditions can be remedied. What this means is that whether you find work or not is your decision. Before you decide, however, you should know the price you pay for extended unemployment. It's very high, and you pay interest on it for a lifetime. Here's what you can expect if you stay unemployed for a long period of time:

- Depression
- Low self-esteem
- Social isolation
- Anger and hostility
- Inability to accept rejection or help
- Deteriorating personal relationships
- Inertia (becoming a "couch potato")
- Poor appearance
- Severe limitations on your life-style
- Bill collectors at your door
- Standing in welfare lines
- Inability to finance a job search
- Loss of job skills
- Mental illness
- Physical illness
- Drug abuse

Reducing the length of your unemployment by even a few weeks will help you avoid some of the depressing events described above. It can also mean lots of dollars in your pocket that would otherwise not be there. Increased happiness and more money—does that sound interesting? If so, you'll be extremely interested in *The Work Book*.

What *The Work Book* Is All About

The development of *The Work Book* began with the authors' attempts to provide job seekers with a proven, simple method for finding work in the shortest possible time and with the least amount of anxiety and fear. To accomplish this the authors began by asking job seekers and professional job-search trainers from all across the country for help. What advice did the authors receive?

- "Keep it simple and brief."
- "Explain what to do and why."
- "Use lots of proven exercises."

As a result of this research, *The Work Book* was designed to meet two objectives:

1. ***To decrease the amount of time you spend looking for work once you actively begin your job search.*** Remember, the average length of time for being unemployed in a good economy is 3–4 months. You can do much better than that if you follow *The Work Book* plan.

2. ***To eliminate much of the fear associated with looking for work and participating in an interview.*** Since fear usually stems from a lack of knowledge and skill, *The Work Book* makes sure that you get a good dose of both.

The Work Book will teach you the skills you need to be more effective, efficient, and productive as a job seeker. It will answer all five of the questions that job seekers are most concerned about:

The Five Basic Job Seeker Questions

1. Where are the jobs?
2. Whom do I talk to?
3. How do I contact these people?
4. What do I say when I contact them?
5. What's the easiest way to convince employers to hire me?

After reading and working through *The Work Book*, you will have no trouble answering these five questions. In fact, you will be among the 5 percent of the population who have been trained to be successful in their job search. You will be able to do the following:

- Meet employer expectations
- Answer key interview questions
- Keep an interview focused on your skills
- Discuss your achievements
- Control your nervousness
- Create job-search networks
- Develop job leads
- Use the phone effectively for contacts
- Actively use the "hidden" job market
- Design a JIST card
- Create resumes and cover letters
- Follow up after an interview
- Prove you are a good risk

Moving Ahead

Before you begin reading and working your way through *The Work Book*—one word of caution. The authors tried their best to write a magical job-search manual. Unfortunately they failed. They were unable to develop the perfect, complete, easy answer for finding everyone his or her dream job instantly. They tried, but they just couldn't do it!

What this means is that you are going to have to do your fair share of the work. You will need to do four things:

1. *Identify a realistic job objective or career goal.* You must know the type of work you want to get the maximum value from this book. Employers rarely hire people who want "anything" jobs.

2. *Take some risks—talk with people.* People hire people! Quite simply, this means that you are going to have to take some interpersonal risks by meeting new people, recontacting "old" acquaintances, and talking with both former and potential employers. Everyone you used to know and everyone you will meet can be of help.

3. *Learn how the labor market and hiring process work.* You must learn the rules of the game if you want to perform better in that game. *The Work Book* is geared toward teaching you how to look for work the smart way instead of looking for work the hard way.

4. *Invest the time and energy needed to make the process work.* If you learn nothing else from *The Work Book*, learn that your economic future is in your hands—and yours alone. No teacher, family member, friend, or counselor can guarantee your career success. It's up to you.

So, now it's decision-making time. You need to decide whether or not the idea of a good living, nice home, emotional stability, strong family ties, and entertaining social life are worth the effort of doing the job-search right. If your answer is "No, it's too much work, too much stress, too much whatever," please give this book to someone who does want some of the nicer things in life. If your answer is "Yes, you better believe it," then let's get started—right now!

1

CHAPTER ONE

Employer Expectations
Measuring Up

You cannot succeed in a job search unless you first make some important decisions. Your decisions should answer two questions: "What do I really want to do?" and "What can I do well?" To answer these questions, think about your career choices as well as your aptitudes and abilities. Think long and hard before you decide.

Knowing what you want to do and can do well should give you a specific career goal, or job objective. Your goal should help you find a job that you will like.

Note that you *cannot* do the work in this text without having a career goal in mind. If you do not have such a goal, get help in defining one for yourself before you go any further.

To be sure that you are in a good position to make use of this text, write the title of the job you want below.

MY JOB OBJECTIVE

_____

Now that you are set on a career goal, try an exercise. Imagine that you are an employer in your field of choice and that you are looking for someone to fill a position like the one you listed above. What would you expect from a good employee?

This is valuable information for you to have as a job seeker. If you know what employers in your field of interest want, you can tailor the way you present yourself to their needs. This will help you convince them that you are the right person for their job.

Knowing what to expect will also enable you to solve some key problems—yours and potential employers':

- *Your problem—job-search jitters.* These are the fears and nervousness you feel when making job inquiries or answering interview questions. Their source? Not knowing what to expect—and a lack of practice.

- *Employers' problem—inability to get good information from applicants during interviews.* This can result from poor interviewing technique on the part of the interviewer, poor presentation by the interviewee, or both.

Continue with your exercise. Imagine you are sitting behind a desk in your private office. You have been interviewing applicants for the position you need to fill. Your secretary is about to bring the next would-be employee into your office. How will you decide whether or not to hire this person? What things will you look for? Write your expectations in the blanks below. Two examples have been provided to get you started.

1. *Good manners*
2. *Willingness to learn*
3. _____
4. _____
5. _____
6. _____
7. _____
8. _____
9. _____
10. _____

There are no wrong answers to the exercise you just completed. As an employer, you are free to follow your personal preferences when choosing employees. But how do you learn as a job seeker what these preferences are?

Learning the particular expectations of particular employers can be difficult. It is not difficult, however, to learn the expectations of employers *in general*. Studies have shown that most employers have three major expectations. In this chapter you will learn what those expectations are and how you can use them to your advantage in seeking a job. The exercises in this chapter will help you show employers how your life, work, and educational experiences match up with these expectations.

Expectation One: Appearance

Do you look like the right person for the job?

You have probably heard about the importance of making a good first impression. Well, the impression you make in a job interview is especially important. If you do not make a good first impression there, your first impression will also be your last.

Even before you shake hands and introduce yourself, an employer begins forming an opinion of you. This is natural. Since you have little time to present yourself, your appearance greatly influences the employer's final opinion. This makes appearance one of the three main employer expectations.

Four aspects of your appearance concern employers. Employers are concerned about your appearance as shown by the way you look, behave, speak, and write. Each type of appearance is just as important as all of the others. If you meet these expectations, your first impression will be a good and lasting one.

The Way You Look

It may seem too obvious to state, but good personal appearance and hygiene are extremely important when you are looking for a job. Many people suffering from extended unemployment stop paying attention to their physical selves. This further prolongs their unemployment. Don't you be one of these people!

When you go to an interview, look like the right person for the job. In the first few seconds, an employer will probably decide not to hire you if you have neglected your personal appearance. It will make no difference how skilled or experienced you are. The employer will usually hire someone who takes care with his or her appearance.

Three factors determine the way you look. These factors are dress, grooming, and hygiene.

Dress An employer will notice immediately how you have dressed for an interview. Here are some basic rules to follow as you plan your attire:

- *Dress one step above what you would actually wear on the job.* For example, if you would wear jeans and a T-shirt on the job, wear nice, casual clothes to the interview. You can find out what kind of clothing is worn on the job by visiting the company beforehand. Notice the dress of employees with jobs similar to the one you are seeking. If it is not possible to observe employees, use your good judgment. After a few interviews, you will have a good idea how to adjust your dress to fit the situation.

- *Wear clothes that are clean, neat, and in good condition.* Buy good-quality, well-fitted clothes and—while you are job hunting—use them for interviews only.

- *Dress conservatively.* Do not wear anything loud, either in terms of color or pattern. Avoid excessive or gaudy jewelry and accessories. Shine your shoes and see that they are in good repair. Take note: if you feel that it's nobody's business but yours what type of clothes you wear, don't expect to be hired right away. The price you pay for wearing extreme or unusual styles may be extended unemployment.

- *Have a "dress rehearsal" before the interview.* Dress exactly as you will for the interview. Then ask a friend or relative for comments. Say, "I'm going to interview for a job as a (fill in the position). Do I look like the right person for the job? Do you think I'm dressed one level above what other people doing this job would wear?" Have your dress rehearsal in front of a mirror if there is no one to give helpful comments.

Now use your common sense and past experiences to decide how you would dress for an interview. Assume the interview is for the job that you want. How will you dress? Give the color and type of clothing for each category.

MY DRESSING PLAN

Shirt/blouse/jacket: _____

_____

Skirt/slacks: _____

Dress/suit: _____

Shoes: _____

Hose/socks: _____

Accessories (jewelry, scarf/tie, belt, etc.): _____

_____

_____

Grooming   Grooming is another part of how you look. You should follow these basic rules:

- *Keep your hair well-groomed.* It should be clean, combed, and neatly styled.

- *Men, shave before an interview; neatly trim and comb mustaches.* If you want to grow a mustache or beard, it's probably a good idea to wait until after you've finished with your interviews. Mustaches and beards in their early stages can be mistaken for poor grooming. Ask yourself if the change is really worth risking the good opinion of a potential employer.

- *Neatly trim and clean your fingernails.* Women who wear fashion nails should consider limiting themselves to moderate lengths and conservative colors. Some employers might worry that more extreme styles would interfere with job tasks or project the wrong business image.

- *Use makeup, perfume, or after-shave sparingly.* In the cosmetic area, it's easy to step over the line into too much of a good thing. Remember that this could distract an interviewer from your assets as an employee. You would be trying to sell yourself, while your interviewer would be wondering how customers or clients might react.

Employers expect the right person for a job to be well-groomed. What does complete grooming include? Explain how you can make sure that you are well-groomed.

MY GROOMING PLAN

Hair: _____

Face: _____

Hands: _____

Other: _____

Hygiene   Hygiene is a third important factor in your appearance. Practice the following basic rules for good personal hygiene:

- Keep your body clean.

- Wash your hair regularly.

- Brush and floss your teeth every day.

- Use a deodorant.

- Clean your fingernails.

Dress, grooming, and hygiene are closely related. Neglect of one hurts the others. Even if you are well dressed and well groomed, you cannot make a good impression if you have overlooked the basics of good personal hygiene.

The Way You Behave

Another part of appearance that employers consider is your manner. Manner refers to your behavior. How you behave in an interview gives the employer an idea of how you might behave on the job. Since you have little time to make an impression, your manner will greatly affect that impression.

Try to conduct yourself during an interview with confidence. Also, be natural and positive—but don't overdo it. Just be yourself. (Honesty and sincerity are also elements of a good manner.) Finally, always show employers common courtesy.

The Way You Write

The third aspect of appearance involves the paperwork you must do to make your job search successful. For example, almost all employers require job seekers to fill out application forms.

You must do your paperwork in a way that shows employers that you are neat, accurate, and thorough. In later chapters, you will learn how to prepare and use various aids to help you do this.

The Way You Speak

Another part of your appearance is the way you speak. Your manner of speaking is most important during interviews and phone contacts. It shows up in practices like these:

- Thinking and organizing your thoughts before speaking

- Talking about results, achievements, and how you can be of help to employers

- Pronouncing words clearly

- Using correct grammar

- Expressing enthusiasm with your voice

- Being open and frank with interviewers (that is, responding readily and directly to their questions)

For whatever reasons, many employers like to hire people with good verbal communication skills. Be one of these people!

Expectation Two: Dependability

Can you be counted on to do the job?

Employers hire people who show the most promise of being at work on time every day. Most companies operate on the idea that time is money. Employees who miss work often or frequently arrive late cannot contribute fully. A highly skilled worker who is absent a great deal will not produce as much as a more dependable worker with fewer skills. Nonproductive employees do not stay employed for long. Such workers often cost a company money rather than help it make a profit.

The second important employer expectation, then, is dependability. Dependability includes two specific qualities—attendance and punctuality. It also includes a general quality—reliability. During all parts of your job search, you must convince employers that you can meet their expectations in these areas.

Attendance

Employers want to hire people who will maintain a good attendance record. Employers expect all workers to be on the job as scheduled. Employees who are at work every day produce more. In this way, they make more money for the company—and for themselves.

During an interview one of your aims is to give the interviewer proof that you have shown good attendance in the past. You can do this with specific examples from your life, work, or educational experiences.

A specific example tells a story by describing some of the *who, what, where, when, why,* and *how* of the example. When you can tell employers exactly when and how you have shown good attendance, you establish your ability to do good work. You also prove that you have invested time and energy preparing for your job search and that you possess the communication skills that employers want.

There are a few basic ways you can show employers that you meet their expectations of good attendance. Note that you have not missed many days at work or at school. If you did miss a few days and made up the work, say so! As a rule of thumb, six missed days a year, without serious illness, are considered acceptable to most employers.

What do you do if you have a poor attendance record? First, try to answer the question *Why?* Then, talk about the situation with a placement counselor or job-search professional. Remember, not having a satisfactory response to a question about your attendance can ruin your chances for a job.

You can reinforce your intention to maintain good attendance by showing employers your attendance records for team practices, club meetings, political activities, or volunteer activities. If you have won an award for attendance, make sure you say so. Such an award would be the best possible evidence of your attendance behavior.

Now, identify three specific examples of your good attendance.

Attendance example 1: _____

_____

Attendance example 2: _____

_____

Attendance example 3: _____

_____

Use your examples to prepare what you will say to employers when the topic of attendance comes up in an interview. Here's a sample of the kind of statement you might make: "I have a pattern of good attendance. I haven't missed an appointment in over a year. I haven't missed a day of work in over six months, and my school attendance was approximately 95 percent." Now write your statement in the space below.

MY ATTENDANCE STATEMENT

_____

_____

_____

_____

_____

_____

_____

An unbelievable number of people miss interviews simply because they forget them. To guard against this, you should keep a written record of your interview appointments. This schedule should show the date, time, location, and name of the interviewer.

Missing an interview tells an employer how little value you place on his or her job and on attendance in general. But suppose you can't keep an appointment for an interview for a legitimate reason? (Perhaps you have unexpected problems with transportation or child care.) Call the employer before the interview. Explain the situation, take responsibility for the problem, and request another interview date. This is not a good situation, but it has happened to others. Your odds of saving the day are fifty-fifty.

Punctuality

Punctuality means being places on time and completing your work on schedule. Here are some examples:

- Getting to work on time when there are difficult circumstances, such as bad weather or car problems

- Coming back from breaks and lunches on time

- Not leaving work or school early

- Meeting school or work assignment deadlines

- Regularly arriving at meetings and appointments on time

- Winning attendance awards at work, clubs, or school

In the spaces below, describe three specific situations in which you demonstrated punctuality. These examples will help you prove to employers that you are a punctual person and a good employment risk.

Punctuality example 1: _____

_____

Punctuality example 2: _____

_____

Punctuality example 3: _____

_____

One of the easiest and most observable ways of showing your interest in punctuality is to show up early for your interviews. Don't arrive too early, however. That may make the interviewer and/or any secretarial personnel uncomfortable. It may also tell the employer that you are too "hungry" for the position. Ten to fifteen minutes early would be about right.

If you have a problem with punctuality, discuss it with your instructor or counselor. Then get started developing appropriate interview answers on the subject.

Here's an example of what you might say if your record is outstanding: "In all the time I was in school, I was never cited for being late for class. This carried over into my work and social life. On occasion, I've even given up breakfast so that I wouldn't be late for work. I can't remember the last time I was late for an appointment."

Now write a brief statement about your punctuality that might impress an interviewer.

MY PUNCTUALITY STATEMENT

_____

_____

_____

_____

Reliability

Excellent attendance and punctuality imply a more general employer expectation—reliability. Reliability means that an employer can count on you to do your job.

Compare yourself with the following descriptions of a reliable worker. Place a check (✓) next to each phrase that you think describes you. If you have never had a job, think of the descriptions in terms of your educational, family, or life situations.

You are a reliable worker if you

_____ put in an honest day's work each day.

_____ learn something new at every opportunity.

_____ get along with co-workers, customers, supervisors, and instructors.

_____ leave your personal problems at home.

_____ follow supervisory directions and company policies.

_____ keep a clean, neat, safe workplace and take care of equipment.

_____ ask for help—but only after you have tried your best to solve the problem.

_____ admit to mistakes and work at improving your weaknesses.

_____ work until the job is done right, even if it means unpaid overtime.

Select the three checked statements above that you feel most comfortable talking about. Then give a brief, specific example of how each one applies to you.

Reliability example 1: _____

_____

Reliability example 2: _____

_____

Reliability example 3: _____

_____

Here is an example of a short statement that a job seeker could use in interviews to establish that he or she is reliable: "You'll find that I'm a reliable worker. On my last job I performed all of my cleaning duties well. Because of this, my boss asked me to be responsible for collecting the money from the pop machines. My tally was always on the mark. Later I was promoted to shift leader for the custodial crew."

Now write a short reliability statement of your own.

MY RELIABILITY STATEMENT

_____

_____

_____

_____

Expectation Three: Skills

What can you do?

Employers usually provide new employees with training for specific jobs. The training is designed to strengthen existing skills or teach new ones. In all cases, however, employers expect each person they hire to already have, or be able to develop, basic job skills. This means that you must have the potential to do the job and that you must express this potential in your job-search documents and personal contacts.

Employers will surely ask about your skills during an interview. They can ask this question in many different ways. Here are some typical examples:

- "What sort of experience do you have?"

- "Why should I hire you?"

- "What do you have to offer?"

- "What do you know about the job?"

- "How did you get your experience?"

- "What do you think makes someone a good worker in this field?"

Many job seekers, like the one in the following example, answer such questions vaguely:

    Employer: "What sort of experience do you have?"

    Job seeker: "Well, I was a secretary at Chrysler for three years and a bon-bon wrapper at Russell's Sweets for two years."

This response does not describe the job seeker's skills specifically. Instead, it mentions two job titles and two periods and places of employment.

Compare this typical response to the one at the top of page 10. The interviewee is seeking a position as a secretary in a music shop.

Employer: "Tell me about your experience."

Job seeker: "Gladly. I have three years' secretarial experience with Chrysler. My skills include keyboarding 60 words per minute accurately, working familiarity with three major word processing programs, good telephone presence, and experience using a variety of fax machines and photocopiers. I also pick up new procedures and filing systems very quickly. My education includes completion of a business-prep curriculum in high school and an associate in arts degree from Yarmouth Business College.

I'm very orderly and efficient about everything that I do. In fact, you could say that I'm a secretary even when it comes to my hobby. I have a collection of over 2,000 phonograph records. I've cataloged it, cross-referencing by artist, title, and composer. My love for music and attention to order come naturally—my father was a librarian and my mother a musician. I learned a great deal from them. I'm sure you would find my work for your company to be excellent."

There is quite a difference between the two preceding examples. The first response barely answers the question; the second response is direct and comprehensive. In this chapter, you will learn how to make statements like the second.

When you answer interview questions about your skills, you should be specific and complete. To do this effectively, you must first learn about your own skills triangle. What is a skills triangle? It is the grouping together of the three kinds of skills employers look for in employees. Everyone has a skills triangle, but most people don't know how to use it to find work. You will soon be one of the few job seekers who do.

Whether employers know it or not, during an interview they want you to talk about three types of skills—job-related skills, transferable skills, and self-management skills. These three types of skills make up your own personal triangle of skills. By identifying your personal skills triangle, you can become a confident and effective job seeker. You can then meet an employer's skills expectations and show him or her that you are a well-rounded individual who will be an excellent worker.

The remaining exercises in this chapter will help you identify and list the skills in your personal skills triangle. In the next chapter you will identify your abilities and experiences in such areas as education, hobbies, and personal successes. After completing these two chapters, you will have lists of specific skills and experiences in each of the following categories:

Your Skills Triangle

- Job-related skills

- Transferable skills

- Self-management skills

- Work experience

- Education and training

- Interests and hobbies

- Life experiences

- Successes and achievements

Transferable Skills

As you develop your lists of skills, make sure that your responses relate to the job you want. In this way you can determine your potential to do that particular job.

Job-Related Skills

Job-related skills are the basic work skills needed to do a good job. Employers ask about such skills during interviews so that they can determine whether or not applicants have a working knowledge of a job.

Job-related skills are discussed using the vocabulary of the particular field of work. For example, carpenters "set rafters," do "trim work," "hang joists," and use "stringers" for stairs. These words would not normally figure in the discussion of a secretarial position. A secretary would be expected to "word process," "schedule appointments," and "keep files."

Sometimes job-related skills are called screening skills because they "screen out" applicants who are unable to show employers that they understand the demands of the position. You should realize that when employers ask you about your experiences, they want to know if you have the basic knowledge and skills to do the job.

Regardless of the type of work you want, all job-related skills fall into four simple categories: data, people, things, and ideas. It's easier to talk about your job-related skills if you think about them in these terms.

Data The category of data involves working with facts, numbers, and other pieces of information. What types of information will you be responsible for in your new job? Some examples are customer files, expense reports, survey data, and delivery schedules. List the kinds of information you will work with in the job you are seeking.

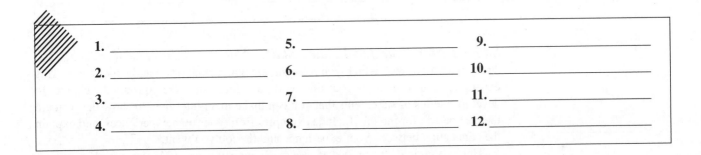

1. _____   5. _____   9. _____
2. _____   6. _____   10. _____
3. _____   7. _____   11. _____
4. _____   8. _____   12. _____

People The category of people involves working with people in different ways. What types of involvement will you have with other people in doing your job? Some examples are meeting customers, handling complaints, counseling children, and supervising others. List the ways in which you will work with people.

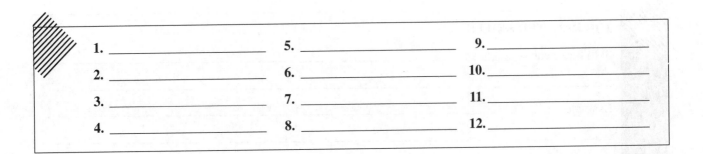

1. _____   5. _____   9. _____
2. _____   6. _____   10. _____
3. _____   7. _____   11. _____
4. _____   8. _____   12. _____

Things The category of things involves working with tools, machines, or equipment. What tools, machines, or equipment will you have to operate on your next job? Some examples are word processor, ohm meter, tape recorder, arc welder, and saw. List the tools, machines, or pieces of equipment that you will probably use.

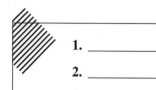

1. _____	5. _____	9. _____
2. _____	6. _____	10. _____
3. _____	7. _____	11. _____
4. _____	8. _____	12. _____

Ideas The category of ideas is involved with creativity. What types of ideas will you need to use or develop to do a good job? Some examples are promotional ideas, organizational schemes, solutions to problems, and inventions. List the ways in which you will use ideas in your job.

1. _____	5. _____	9. _____
2. _____	6. _____	10. _____
3. _____	7. _____	11. _____
4. _____	8. _____	12. _____

Summarizing Your Job-Related Skills Now go back over the four listings and circle every item with which you have already had actual or related experience. (This experience can come from your life, work, or education.) Use your circled choices to develop a series of statements that you can make in an interview to show that you are the best person for the job. Include examples from your own experiences, and explain the connection between your experience and the job you want.

Here's a sample: "I can do database management on any IBM-compatible computer *(things)*. On my last job, I mastered the Paradox® program *(things)* well enough to maintain, track, and generate reports on over 50 customer accounts *(data)*. I performed this task so effectively that I was asked to instruct other employees in the use of the software *(people)*. Subsequently, I devised a system to help company personnel keep up on new or faster applications of the program to the company's business *(ideas)*. Since the computers and software are the same, I'm sure I could do as well organizing and maintaining your account files." Now use the forms that follow to frame your own statements.

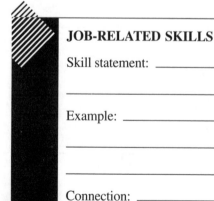

JOB-RELATED SKILLS

Skill statement: _____

_____

Example: _____

_____

_____

Connection: _____

_____

_____

JOB-RELATED SKILLS

Skill statement: _____

_____

Example: _____

_____

_____

Connection: _____

_____

_____

JOB-RELATED SKILLS

Skill statement: _____

_____

Example: _____

_____

_____

Connection: _____

_____

_____

Transferable Skills

Unlike job-related skills, which tend to be used only in one type of work, transferable skills can be used in every occupation. They are universal skills. You can transfer them from one type of work to another without much effort on your part or training from an employer. For this reason, your transferable skills are often more important than your job-related skills. This is especially true if you are changing careers or making the transition from school to work.

Suppose that an automobile mechanic wants a job repairing household appliances. In interviews and applications, the mechanic would emphasize general mechanical skills, not automotive skills. Why? The owner of an appliance repair business would be interested in whether or not an applicant could troubleshoot, repair, adjust, and maintain mechanical devices. Such an employer would not care if an applicant could grind pistons, rebuild carburetors, or adjust ignition timing.

In identifying your transferable skills, do not overlook the skills you have gained from everyday living. Most job seekers fail to see this potential. These skills can, however, help you meet an employer's expectations.

If you do not already know your transferable skills, complete the checklist on pages 14–15. It will help you to identify them.

Transferable Skills Checklist

Review this list of transferable skills and check (✓) all of the skills that you feel you have. Check the Education column if you acquired that skill during your education or through a training program. Check the Life column if you acquired the skill anywhere else, which would include paid employment, volunteer activities, and general life experience. Check the third column, Next Job, if you feel you will need that skill in the next job you have that meets your primary job objective.

Education	Life	Next Job		Education	Life	Next Job		Education	Life	Next Job	
❏	❏	❏	act/perform	❏	❏	❏	correspond w/ others	❏	❏	❏	generate
❏	❏	❏	adapt to situations	❏	❏	❏	create	❏	❏	❏	guide/lead
❏	❏	❏	advise people	❏	❏	❏	delegate	❏	❏	❏	handle complaints
❏	❏	❏	analyze data	❏	❏	❏	deliver	❏	❏	❏	handle equipment
❏	❏	❏	anticipate problems	❏	❏	❏	demonstrate	❏	❏	❏	handle money
❏	❏	❏	appraise service	❏	❏	❏	design	❏	❏	❏	help people
❏	❏	❏	arrange functions	❏	❏	❏	detail	❏	❏	❏	illustrate
❏	❏	❏	assemble products	❏	❏	❏	detect	❏	❏	❏	imagine solutions
❏	❏	❏	assess situations	❏	❏	❏	determine	❏	❏	❏	implement
❏	❏	❏	audit records	❏	❏	❏	develop	❏	❏	❏	improve
❏	❏	❏	bargain/barter	❏	❏	❏	direct others	❏	❏	❏	improvise
❏	❏	❏	be cost conscious	❏	❏	❏	dispense information	❏	❏	❏	inform people
❏	❏	❏	be responsible for	❏	❏	❏	distribute	❏	❏	❏	initiate actions
❏	❏	❏	budget money	❏	❏	❏	do precision work	❏	❏	❏	inspect products
❏	❏	❏	build	❏	❏	❏	do public relations work	❏	❏	❏	install
❏	❏	❏	buy products/services	❏	❏	❏	draft	❏	❏	❏	instruct
❏	❏	❏	calculate numbers	❏	❏	❏	drive	❏	❏	❏	interpret data
❏	❏	❏	chart information	❏	❏	❏	edit	❏	❏	❏	interview people
❏	❏	❏	check for accuracy	❏	❏	❏	encourage	❏	❏	❏	invent
❏	❏	❏	classify information	❏	❏	❏	endure long hours	❏	❏	❏	inventory
❏	❏	❏	collect money	❏	❏	❏	enforce	❏	❏	❏	investigate
❏	❏	❏	communicate	❏	❏	❏	entertain	❏	❏	❏	lead people
❏	❏	❏	compare data	❏	❏	❏	establish	❏	❏	❏	learn
❏	❏	❏	compile statistics	❏	❏	❏	estimate	❏	❏	❏	learn quickly
❏	❏	❏	compute data	❏	❏	❏	evaluate	❏	❏	❏	liaise
❏	❏	❏	conceptualize	❏	❏	❏	examine	❏	❏	❏	lift (heavy)
❏	❏	❏	conduct	❏	❏	❏	exchange	❏	❏	❏	lift (moderate)
❏	❏	❏	confront others	❏	❏	❏	exhibit	❏	❏	❏	listen
❏	❏	❏	construct buildings	❏	❏	❏	expand	❏	❏	❏	locate information
❏	❏	❏	consult w/ others	❏	❏	❏	expedite	❏	❏	❏	log information
❏	❏	❏	contact others	❏	❏	❏	explain	❏	❏	❏	make/create
❏	❏	❏	contact w/ others	❏	❏	❏	explore	❏	❏	❏	make decisions
❏	❏	❏	control costs	❏	❏	❏	file records	❏	❏	❏	make policy
❏	❏	❏	control people	❏	❏	❏	find information	❏	❏	❏	manage a business
❏	❏	❏	control situations	❏	❏	❏	fix/repair	❏	❏	❏	manage people
❏	❏	❏	converse w/ others	❏	❏	❏	follow directions	❏	❏	❏	measure boundaries
❏	❏	❏	coordinate activities	❏	❏	❏	follow through	❏	❏	❏	mediate problems
❏	❏	❏	cope w/ deadlines	❏	❏	❏	gather information	❏	❏	❏	meet the public
❏	❏	❏	copy information	❏	❏	❏	gather materials	❏	❏	❏	memorize information

Transferable Skills Checklist (continued)

Education	Life	Next Job		Education	Life	Next Job		Education	Life	Next Job	
❏	❏	❏	mentor others	❏	❏	❏	refer people	❏	❏	❏	synthesize
❏	❏	❏	monitor progress	❏	❏	❏	rehabilitate people	❏	❏	❏	tabulate
❏	❏	❏	motivate others	❏	❏	❏	remember information	❏	❏	❏	take instructions
❏	❏	❏	move materials	❏	❏	❏	remove	❏	❏	❏	tend equipment
❏	❏	❏	negotiate	❏	❏	❏	repair	❏	❏	❏	test
❏	❏	❏	nurse	❏	❏	❏	replace	❏	❏	❏	think ahead
❏	❏	❏	nurture	❏	❏	❏	report information	❏	❏	❏	think logically
❏	❏	❏	observe	❏	❏	❏	research	❏	❏	❏	tolerate interruptions
❏	❏	❏	obtain	❏	❏	❏	resolve problems	❏	❏	❏	track
❏	❏	❏	operate equipment	❏	❏	❏	restore	❏	❏	❏	train/teach
❏	❏	❏	order goods/supplies	❏	❏	❏	retrieve information	❏	❏	❏	transcribe
❏	❏	❏	organize data	❏	❏	❏	review	❏	❏	❏	transfer
❏	❏	❏	organize people	❏	❏	❏	run meetings	❏	❏	❏	translate
❏	❏	❏	organize tasks	❏	❏	❏	schedule	❏	❏	❏	travel
❏	❏	❏	own/operate business	❏	❏	❏	seek out	❏	❏	❏	treat/provide care
❏	❏	❏	paint	❏	❏	❏	select	❏	❏	❏	troubleshoot
❏	❏	❏	perceive needs	❏	❏	❏	sell	❏	❏	❏	tutor
❏	❏	❏	perform routine work	❏	❏	❏	separate	❏	❏	❏	type
❏	❏	❏	persuade others	❏	❏	❏	sequence	❏	❏	❏	understand
❏	❏	❏	plan	❏	❏	❏	service customers	❏	❏	❏	unite people
❏	❏	❏	plant	❏	❏	❏	service equipment	❏	❏	❏	update information
❏	❏	❏	prepare materials	❏	❏	❏	set goals/objectives	❏	❏	❏	upgrade
❏	❏	❏	print	❏	❏	❏	set up equipment	❏	❏	❏	use hand-eye
❏	❏	❏	process information	❏	❏	❏	set up systems				coordination
❏	❏	❏	process materials	❏	❏	❏	sew	❏	❏	❏	use words correctly
❏	❏	❏	produce	❏	❏	❏	shape/mold	❏	❏	❏	verify
❏	❏	❏	program	❏	❏	❏	signal	❏	❏	❏	visit
❏	❏	❏	promote	❏	❏	❏	size up situations	❏	❏	❏	visualize
❏	❏	❏	protect property	❏	❏	❏	sketch	❏	❏	❏	volunteer
❏	❏	❏	provide maintenance	❏	❏	❏	socialize	❏	❏	❏	weigh
❏	❏	❏	question others	❏	❏	❏	solve problems	❏	❏	❏	work quickly
❏	❏	❏	raise money	❏	❏	❏	sort	❏	❏	❏	write procedures
❏	❏	❏	read reference books	❏	❏	❏	speak in public	❏	❏	❏	write promo material
❏	❏	❏	recommend	❏	❏	❏	study	❏	❏	❏	write proposals
❏	❏	❏	record data	❏	❏	❏	supervise	❏	❏	❏	write reports
❏	❏	❏	recruit people	❏	❏	❏	supply	❏	❏	❏	write technical work
❏	❏	❏	rectify	❏	❏	❏	support				
❏	❏	❏	reduce costs	❏	❏	❏	survey				

Once you have identified your transferable skills, you will need to develop them into the same kind of statements you prepared for your job-related skills. Here are some samples.

- *Transferable skill statement:* "I can meet deadlines."

    Example: "While in school, I rarely missed a due date on an assignment."

    Connection: "If I was able to meet deadlines in school, I will also be able to meet your work deadlines."

- *Transferable skill statement:* "I can keep financial records."

    Example: "As a full-time homemaker, I handled all of the family money, including savings and checking accounts, without ever bouncing a check or failing to pay a bill on time."

    Connection: "If I could handle the family finances so well for 20 years, while taking care of all of the other household chores at the same time, I could be a good account clerk for you."

- *Transferable skill statement:* "I'm a well-organized person."

    Example: "At my last job I had six bosses. I had to organize my time and set priorities to get the job done to everyone's satisfaction."

    Connection: "If I could handle that confusion, I'm sure I'll be able to deal with the organizational demands of this job."

Now choose the three transferable skills from your list that you think will most interest potential employers. Develop these skills into complete statements using the forms that follow.

TRANSFERABLE SKILLS

Skill statement: _____

_____

Example: _____

_____

_____

Connection: _____

_____

TRANSFERABLE SKILLS

Skill statement: _____

_____

Example: _____

_____

_____

Connection: _____

_____

TRANSFERABLE SKILLS

Skill statement: _____

_____

Example: _____

_____

_____

Connection: _____

_____

Self-Management Skills

Self-management skills make up the last part of your skills triangle. These skills tell an employer if you will get along well with workers and managers already on the job. Over half of all employees who are unsuccessful on the job have trouble with their co-workers or bosses. Such personality conflicts damage morale and can interfere with productivity. They cost employers time, aggravation, and money. So, it's important for you to show potential employers how well you would fit into their operations. Many businesses would rather hire an inexperienced worker with good self-management skills than an experienced one who might cause problems.

If you are not sure what self-management skills you have, complete the checklist that follows. It will help you identify them.

Self-Management Skills Checklist

Review this list of self-management skills and check (✓) any three that you believe you exhibit over 50 percent of the time. Place a second check next to the ten skills that you believe would be most important in your next job.

I Exhibit	Next Job		I Exhibit	Next Job		I Exhibit	Next Job	
❑	❑	academic	❑	❑	clever	❑	❑	easygoing
❑	❑	accurate	❑	❑	competent	❑	❑	efficient
❑	❑	active	❑	❑	competitive	❑	❑	emotional
❑	❑	adaptable	❑	❑	confident	❑	❑	energetic
❑	❑	adventurous	❑	❑	conscientious	❑	❑	enterprising
❑	❑	affectionate	❑	❑	conservative	❑	❑	enthusiastic
❑	❑	aggressive	❑	❑	considerate	❑	❑	fair-minded
❑	❑	alert	❑	❑	cool	❑	❑	farsighted
❑	❑	ambitious	❑	❑	cooperative	❑	❑	firm
❑	❑	artistic	❑	❑	courageous	❑	❑	flexible
❑	❑	assertive	❑	❑	creative	❑	❑	forceful
❑	❑	attractive	❑	❑	curious	❑	❑	formal
❑	❑	bold	❑	❑	daring	❑	❑	frank
❑	❑	broad-minded	❑	❑	deliberate	❑	❑	friendly
❑	❑	businesslike	❑	❑	democratic	❑	❑	generous
❑	❑	calm	❑	❑	dependable	❑	❑	gentle
❑	❑	careful	❑	❑	determined	❑	❑	good-natured
❑	❑	cautious	❑	❑	dignified	❑	❑	healthy
❑	❑	charming	❑	❑	discreet	❑	❑	helpful
❑	❑	cheerful	❑	❑	dominant	❑	❑	honest
❑	❑	clear-thinking	❑	❑	eager	❑	❑	humorous

Self-Management Skills Checklist (continued)

I Exhibit	Next Job		I Exhibit	Next Job		I Exhibit	Next Job	
❏	❏	idealistic	❏	❏	peaceable	❏	❏	sociable
❏	❏	imaginative	❏	❏	persevering	❏	❏	spontaneous
❏	❏	independent	❏	❏	pleasant	❏	❏	spunky
❏	❏	individualistic	❏	❏	poised	❏	❏	stable
❏	❏	industrious	❏	❏	polite	❏	❏	steady
❏	❏	informal	❏	❏	practical	❏	❏	strong
❏	❏	ingenious	❏	❏	precise	❏	❏	strong-minded
❏	❏	intellectual	❏	❏	productive	❏	❏	sympathetic
❏	❏	intelligent	❏	❏	progressive	❏	❏	tactful
❏	❏	kind	❏	❏	prudent	❏	❏	teachable
❏	❏	leisurely	❏	❏	punctual	❏	❏	tenacious
❏	❏	lighthearted	❏	❏	purposeful	❏	❏	thorough
❏	❏	likable	❏	❏	quick	❏	❏	thoughtful
❏	❏	logical	❏	❏	quiet	❏	❏	tolerant
❏	❏	loyal	❏	❏	rational	❏	❏	tough
❏	❏	mature	❏	❏	realistic	❏	❏	trusting
❏	❏	methodical	❏	❏	reasonable	❏	❏	trustworthy
❏	❏	meticulous	❏	❏	reflective	❏	❏	unaffected
❏	❏	mild	❏	❏	relaxed	❏	❏	unassuming
❏	❏	moderate	❏	❏	reliable	❏	❏	understanding
❏	❏	modest	❏	❏	reserved	❏	❏	unexcitable
❏	❏	natural	❏	❏	resourceful	❏	❏	uninhibited
❏	❏	obliging	❏	❏	responsible	❏	❏	verbal
❏	❏	open-minded	❏	❏	retiring	❏	❏	versatile
❏	❏	opportunistic	❏	❏	robust	❏	❏	warm
❏	❏	optimistic	❏	❏	self-confident	❏	❏	wholesome
❏	❏	organized	❏	❏	sensible	❏	❏	wise
❏	❏	original	❏	❏	sensitive	❏	❏	witty
❏	❏	outgoing	❏	❏	serious	❏	❏	zany
❏	❏	painstaking	❏	❏	sharp-witted			
❏	❏	patient	❏	❏	sincere			

Now select three of your strongest self-management skills and develop them into complete statements, including supporting examples. Conclude by showing a connection between each of your skills and the job you want. Use the forms that follow.

SELF-MANAGEMENT SKILLS

Skill statement: _____

_____

Example: _____

_____

_____

Connection: _____

_____

SELF-MANAGEMENT SKILLS

Skill statement: _____

_____

Example: _____

_____

_____

Connection: _____

_____

SELF-MANAGEMENT SKILLS

Skill statement: _____

_____

Example: _____

_____

_____

Connection: _____

_____

CHAPTER TWO

The DataTrakt®
A Pocket Full of Power

To conduct an effective job search, you must know a great many details about yourself, your former employers, and your references. These "details" include dates, phone numbers, addresses, and much more. To get such things right when it counts, you must write them down. Too many job seekers try to rely on memory alone, and too often their memories fail them. When filling out an application or answering interview questions, they forget the simplest information. Nothing makes a worse impression.

But make no mistake—this type of information *is* easy to forget. If you find this hard to believe, take this little quiz:

- Have you ever forgotten a phone number, address, or zip code?

- Have you ever forgotten test answers that you knew the day before?

- Have you ever forgotten the names of people you just met?

- Can you recite the phone numbers, addresses, and zip codes of your former employers and references?

If you still don't believe that your poor memory is your enemy, try another exercise. Read the following phone number and address—*once*. Then try to repeat it accurately.

1-490-876-3982
2175 N. Highland Blvd.
San Francisco, CA 93120

If you had difficulty with this no-stress exercise, just think how much trouble you would have in a pressure situation like an interview. How much of a problem is this? Fully 90 percent of people suffering from extended unemployment can't remember enough about themselves to answer interview questions. Eighty percent have trouble identifying and discussing their skills.

How to Make a Memory Aid

Unlike untrained job seekers, however, you can overcome the memory problem. How? By keeping track of your job-search data with the DataTrakt booklet bound into this text. Open the back cover now and tear out your DataTrakt.

Your DataTrakt will provide you with a foundation for effective job seeking. Once it is filled out, the booklet will serve as an organized record of the information employers want to know. Your education, work history, and other important data will all be included. With the DataTrakt in your pocket or purse, you can just copy this information into an application, without mistakes, deletions, or crossing out. You can also quickly refresh your memory during or before an interview.

In later chapters you will learn to use other job-search tools. These include job applications, JIST cards, resumes, telephone contacts, and interviews. All, however, will be based on the information in your DataTrakt. So, take special care in filling it out. It will save you time and effort later.

Before assembling your DataTrakt, find a quiet place to work. Have handy the personal records that you have saved over the years. You should also have access to a telephone and a phone book, since you may need to gather more data. Use a pencil and get a good no-mark eraser so that you can make neat corrections. When you have a place to work and the recommended supplies, you may continue.

Your job search will require a great deal of personal information. Different employers ask different things, but most of your information will be of interest to every employer. The following list outlines the general areas of personal data commonly required by employers:

- Personal identification

- Work experience

- Education and training

- Job-related personal information

- References

As you read each section in this chapter, print your data in the spaces provided in your own DataTrakt. When an item does not relate to you, put a dash (—) in the appropriate space. If any section poses a problem, or if you believe one of your answers might make a negative impression on an employer, follow this three-step procedure:

1. Leave those items blank.
2. Turn to the same section in the Applications chapter (Chapter 3) to see if the problem is addressed there.
3. Ask your instructor for help.

Hopefully, once you have done further reading or obtained help, you will be able to find a satisfactory response or a solution to your problem. Under no circumstances, however, should you ever write anything negative in your DataTrakt!

Personal Identification

The Personal Identification section of your DataTrakt will contain your basic personal data. The major entries are listed below. Read the instructions that accompany them, and print the data in your DataTrakt.

Name

Print your complete name. Include first name, middle name or initial, and last name. When transferring this information to an application, be sure to sequence it as requested. Some application forms ask for last name first, others for first name.

Social Security Number

Print your social security number. Be sure the number is correct. If you do not have a social security number, apply for one now. You can call or visit your nearest social security office for an application (Form SS-5).

Present Address

Print your present address. Include the street address (and unit number, if applicable); RFD or box number; city, state, and zip code.

Many applications also ask how long have you lived at that address. This information is supposed to indicate how stable and reliable you are. (In other words, if you have lived in one place for a long time, you most likely have roots in the community. There is also a good chance that you have been making regular rent or mortgage payments.) Fill in the length of time you have lived at your present address in years and months.

Other Addresses

Some employers request your previous address as well and the length of time you lived there. This entry could be especially helpful if you have only lived at your present address for a short period of time. Other employers, especially those that hire students, distinguish between permanent (home) and temporary (school) addresses.

Telephone Number

Print your home phone number, area code first. If no one is there during the day to answer this phone, you would be wise to invest in a phone-answering machine. That way, you will not miss out on any job opportunities.

If you do not have a home phone, list the number of a reliable friend or relative who can take your messages. Be sure this person knows that potential employers may be calling.

Finally, if you are new to a community or between residences, you might want to investigate fax or electronic-mail services. These may be available through businesses like Mail Boxes Etc. as well as some shelters and similar charitable agencies. Provided you check in regularly, both faxes and electronic mail can allow you to respond to an inquiry within 24 hours.

Birth Information

You should have little or no occasion to provide this kind of information until after you have been hired. Most companies have removed birth dates and related entries from their applications to conform with antidiscrimination laws.

The one exception involves teenaged job seekers. They may be asked to provide a birth date or an age level (as "under 18"). If they are under 18, they may also be asked to provide proof that they are old enough to work. Proof usually takes the form of a valid work permit.

In your DataTrakt, check the appropriate box to indicate your age level. Also, if necessary, indicate whether or not you have a valid work permit.

Physical Characteristics

Some jobs (like police officer or fire fighter) have height and/or weight requirements. To be legitimate, such restrictions must be job-related—that is, they must be required for the performance of an essential job function. If they are not, they could be seen as discrimination based on gender, age, ethnicity, etc.

Enter your height and weight in the appropriate spaces. Since height is usually expressed in both feet and inches, include both figures. You may use either words or symbols (5 ft. 7 in. or 5' 7") if the application does not specify one or the other.

Citizenship

Check the appropriate space if you are a U.S. citizen. If you are not a citizen, list your visa number and explain the type of visa you have.

Eligibility to Work

As soon as you are hired by an employer, you will have to prove that you are legally entitled to work in the United States. To do this, you must produce one or more documents specified by law. Knowing that this is likely to be one of a new employer's earliest requests, you should plan now how you will comply. You should choose and obtain the documents you will use as proof of your eligibility to work.

Among the best forms of proof are these: a valid U.S. or foreign passport, a certificate of U.S. citizenship, a certificate of naturalization, or an alien registration card (also known as a green card). Any one of these will constitute all the proof you need. If you do not have any of these documents, you can substitute pairs of documents. For example, you could use a driver's license or a military identification card plus a social security card, birth certificate, or INS (Immigration and Naturalization Service) employment authorization form. For a full listing of acceptable documents and document combinations, see your DataTrakt. Once you have reviewed the listing, note the documents you will use.

Emergency Information

Print your data about whom to notify in an emergency. List that person's name, relationship to you, home address, home phone, work address, and work phone. (*Note:* Space for these entries can be found in the DataTrakt section titled Job-Related Personal Information.)

Work Experience

Work experience refers to specific data about past jobs. This information includes the names of former employers and the period of employment for each job. It also includes the titles of positions held and the skills required to do the job.

The Work Experience section is one of the most important parts of your DataTrakt. In this section, you will record the many skills, abilities, and experiences you have to offer by analyzing and evaluating the work you've done in the past. Your job search will depend heavily on this information.

You should take extra care in preparing the Work Experience section of your DataTrakt. Be sure the information you include is accurate and complete. You may need to search through your personal records. You may also need to thumb through the phone book or call directory assistance. You should ask former employers for any data you have difficulty remembering. Estimate only as a last resort.

When you have finished filling out your DataTrakt, you will have a well-developed, positive outline of your work history. This in itself will put you ahead of the average job seeker. You will also find this information useful in many phases of your job search.

Suppose you don't have much work experience? Don't be overly concerned. You will learn later how to emphasize other qualifications.

Basic Information

There are three kinds of work experience: paid, unpaid (volunteer), and military. Before you begin, note that your DataTrakt contains blank forms for only four paid jobs, one volunteer job, and one military job. If you will need more forms for any of these categories, make copies *before* you use the last form.

Print your own work experience data in your DataTrakt. Start with your most recent job and work backward. (In other words, information on your most recent job would go on the form for Job 1. Information on the first job you ever had might go on the form for Job 4.) As you enter your information, make a point of being neat. It's good practice for filling out applications in an employer's office.

Complete one work experience form in your DataTrakt for each work experience you've had, regardless of how long you worked at the job or the type of work you did. If you worked as a volunteer, treat that experience just as if it were a paid position. Do the same with your military experience if you have been in the military.

Most of the work experience forms in the DataTrakt ask you to provide the same basic information. First fill in the employer's name, address, and phone number. Then specify the position you held and the dates of your employment. For other entries, follow the tips below.

Supervisor List the name and title of the supervisor who knows your work best and will give you a good recommendation. If that supervisor is no longer with the company, use the name of someone who knows your work and is willing to act as your work reference.

Note that as a courtesy (and a matter of self-interest), you should contact this person before you use his or her name. Explain the kind of work you are now seeking and how you think your former job supports this goal. Also, try to gauge what the person will say about you in key areas like dependability, job performance, and work relations. If there are any problems, you may be able to smooth things over at this point. If not, at least you will be forewarned and can be ready to respond to interview questions on the subject.

Days Missed This is another entry often missing from today's job applications. Most kinds of inquiries about absences run afoul of antidiscrimination statutes. Questions about days missed for illness, for example, are prohibited by the Americans with Disabilities Act. Questions about days lost to child care problems—especially if asked of women only—could constitute gender discrimination. For these reasons, most employers don't ask about attendance at all on job applications.

Note, however, that the subject will certainly come up as part of a thoroughgoing reference check. It might even occur in some form in an interview. (In fact, if your attendance record is good, you may want to bring it up yourself!) If you have over six days of missed time per year, be prepared to discuss the matter in an interview.

Reason for Leaving Pay close attention to how you word your responses here. Do not write negative comments. Negative information on an application or in an interview may cause employers to doubt your value as an employee, even if your other qualities are outstanding. *Never* state your reason for leaving a position with phrases like these:

- "I quit."

- "I was fired."

- "I was terminated."

- "I had problems with the boss."

- "I had problems with co-workers."

- "The pay was too low."

- "The work was too hard."

- "The job was too dirty."

- "I was arrested."

Whatever your reason for leaving a job, you should list only positive information in your DataTrakt. The examples highlighted below may help you state your reasons for leaving in the most favorable terms.

Reasons for Leaving

- "I desired a more challenging position."
- "I had an opportunity for a better job."
- "I wanted to be more productive."
- "I wanted a position with responsibility."
- "I wanted a job requiring my best skills."
- "I wanted work that was career-oriented."
- "I made a long-planned move to this area."
- "There was a general layoff in the plant."
- "The work was seasonal (part time)."
- "I preferred a better work environment."
- "I wanted a job in which I could learn."
- "I became a full-time student."
- "I began a long-planned tour of the United States."
- "I began self-employment."
- "I desire a career-oriented position in (field in which you are applying)."

When you have finished all of your work experience forms, go back and check the flow of your Reason for Leaving entries. Start at the end of your list. Does your reason for leaving Job 4 support your having taken Job 3? Does your reason for leaving Job 3 support your having taken Job 2? Continue this questioning. Finally, the reason you left your last job should support your present job search.

Supervisory Duties Employers place special value on employees who can oversee the work of others. If you have ever supervised anyone in a work situation, either formally or informally, enter the number of people you supervised and the duties those workers performed.

Data, People, Things, and Ideas   As you learned in Chapter 1, you can divide all work into four skills categories: data, people, things, and ideas. You will use these categories to collect and organize your work experience information. Notice that in your DataTrakt forms there are boxed areas carrying these labels. Here is what you list in each area:

- ***Data.*** List the ways in which you have used information, such as keeping time-card records, scheduling appointments, and keeping customer files.

- ***People.*** List the people-oriented duties you've had, such as taking customer orders, working as a member of a team or group, and training new workers.

- ***Things.*** List the different kinds of work you've done with equipment such as computers, nail guns, and ohm meters.

- ***Ideas.*** List the creative ideas you've had that have helped your employers, such as devising a more efficient filing system or suggesting an improvement in a product or service.

For each category, list every possible experience you have had. Then, after completing each list, place a check in the NJ (Next Job) column by each item that you think will be relevant to the position you are seeking. You will want to focus on these things when you prepare for interviews.

Other Duties and Responsibilities   Reliable workers do more than their job descriptions demand. You can call attention to your reliability by identifying and listing any duties not already included in your work experience forms.

Also, list any responsibilities you have been assigned. A responsibility is a special duty, such as opening and closing the store, purchasing materials, or training workers. Employers give responsibilities only to the most reliable and skilled workers. List any situations in which you have had more responsibility than your co-workers.

As you complete this final listing, be sure to check the NJ box, if appropriate. Again, these are the duties you will focus on in applications and interviews.

Problem Situations

You learned back in the discussion of reasons for leaving that how you present information is extremely important to the message it conveys. The same situation can be described in either positive or negative terms. In a job search, positive is always favored.

Some forms of information, however, seem less susceptible to having a particular "spin" put on them. Dates and figures fall into this category. So does missing information. Since problems with both are common in job searches, you should anticipate and plan for them.

Limited Work History   What do you do in an application or interview if you have little or no work experience? You make your education part of your work history. In other words, you evaluate your education just as if it were a job. This process is not easy, but it is worth it.

The process works especially well if you are or have been a vocational student. Review your lists of transferable and self-management skills from Chapter 1 for ideas. For example, you could evaluate the work you did as a homemaker just as if it were a business or a paying job. Most homemakers plan, budget, organize, supervise, and instruct—all of which are skills desired by employers.

Job Gaps   A job gap is a period of unemployment between jobs. If you have job gaps in your work history, they are likely to show up when you fill in your employment dates on a job application.

When no reason is given for a job gap, employers can only guess why the job seeker was unemployed for so long. They might think that the gap resulted from the job seeker's being judged unworthy by other employers. Any unexplained job gap will suggest, at the very least, that the applicant's qualifications are less than those expected by an employer.

If you have a job gap of three or more months in your employment history, there are several ways to handle it. Which way you use depends on what you did during that time.

If you did something that employers might find acceptable, say so. This is called the good-excuse method. It works because it shows potential employers that you did something constructive with your time. The method is especially effective if the activity involved was a worthy one that cannot be done while working full time. For example, you may have done such things as baby-sitting, yard work, or house painting, all of which could be considered self-employment. If you took a trip, it could be listed as travel. If you obtained any type of schooling, it could be listed as education. Whatever the good excuse, include it in the DataTrakt.

It is much better to have a positive explanation for your job gap than no explanation at all. Therefore, think carefully about what you did during that time. If you are not sure whether or not the reason sounds positive, ask for opinions.

If you have a job gap and no positive explanation, do not falsify your employment dates. You could lose your new job as a result. Instead, list the information in a slightly different form. You can explain this in an interview, if necessary. For example, Erin Martin has the following job history:

Job 3:   Employed from ___3-90___ to ___4-92___

Job 4:   Employed from ___12-88___ to ___11-89___

Notice that between the end of Job 4 (11-89) and the beginning of Job 3 (3-90), there is a gap of four months. To avoid showing this gap, she should use a technique called stretching. Two forms of stretching are illustrated below.

Job 3   Employed from ___Spring 1990___ to ___Spring 1992___

Job 4   Employed from ___Winter 1988___ to ___Winter 1989___

or

Job 3   Employed from ___1990___ to ___1992___

Job 4   Employed from ___1988___ to ___1989___

The blank method (omitting dates) can also be used to make job gaps less obvious. This method works best for gaps of six months or longer. Here is an example:

Job 3   Employed from ___6-90___ to ___4-92___

Job 4   Employed from _____ to _____

Note that all other data for Job 4 should be listed. If you use the blank method on an application, be prepared to discuss the subject in an interview.

Work Experience Statement

Employers generally expect you to describe your experience on applications and during interviews. Read the following examples of effective work experience statements.

- "I worked at Huron Metalworks for three years as a welder. I am skilled in precision fabrication and am able to both torch and arc weld. I'm sure I will be an excellent welder for you."

- "During the past four years I have been the Assistant Recreations Director at Sunrise Manor Retirement Village. This experience has given me practical insight into the needs and concerns of the elderly. I know that I communicate well with retirement-age people. I will be a dependable member of your Senior Citizens' Hot Line staff."

- "I've worked at McCall's Family Restaurant for the past three years. I began as a busboy and quickly progressed to overseeing the restaurant's salad bar. Later I was made responsible for the stockroom. I also filled in at the cash register. During the past two years I have been in charge of inventory and ordering. As the assistant manager of your cafe, I believe my varied experience would be most valuable."

Now write a work experience statement of your own. Choose the job listed in your DataTrakt that best showcases the skills you have that are related to the job you want. Your statement should contain at least three sentences. The first sentence should include your former employer's name. It should also include the length of time on the job and your title. The second sentence should mention some skills gained from the former job that are related to the job you want now. The third sentence should explain the connection between this past experience and the job you are seeking. The examples above will help you if you're not sure what to write.

MY WORK EXPERIENCE STATEMENT

_____

_____

_____

_____

_____

_____

Education and Training

Formal education and training is more important in some jobs than others. An employer may expect you to have a certain kind of education and training. This could include grammar school, high school, and college. It could also include technical school, business college, and military training.

Basic Information

Make sure that your education and training are completely described in your DataTrakt. For each of the listed levels, provide the following information:

- *Type of school.* The column headed School lists the schools you are likely to have attended. Note the lower boxes marked Other. In these spaces you should list any technical, business, or correspondence schools in which you enrolled. You should also list any programs in which you took part.

- *School name and address.* In the second column, print the name, street address, city, state, and zip code of each school you attended.

- **Dates.** State the month and year that you started and finished at each school.

- **Full time or part time.** Place a check in the column (full time or part time) that best describes your schedule at each school.

- **Fields of study and special courses.** Your high school studies may have been general, business, trades, or college prep. For colleges and other schools, state your major (and minor, if it applies to the job you are seeking).

- **Number of hours completed.** Make this entry only if you did not receive a diploma or degree. Give the number of hours (months, years, semesters, semester hours, or quarter hours) completed when you left the school.

- **Diploma or degree.** If you graduated from high school, write *diploma* in this space. If you graduated from college, include the type of degree and field of study. (An example would be A.A., Commercial Art.) Also, list any degree, diploma, certificate, license, or award received for completing other courses or training programs.

- **Grade point average.** Your grade point average is your average grade for all the courses you took in a certain school. Always include the scale for evaluating the average (for example, 3.0 on a 4-point scale).

- **GED.** If you have a General Education Diploma (GED), print the date you received it. Then print the name and address of the institution where you earned it.

- **Highest grade completed.** At the bottom of the chart, indicate the number of the last full year of school you successfully completed. For example, if you left high school during your senior year, circle 11, the last full year completed.

Your completed chart should resemble the one below. Note the overall neatness of the form and the clarity of the printing. Remember, your DataTrakt provides not only information for job applications but practice in filling them out as well.

EDUCATION & TRAINING

School	Name of School and Complete Address	From mo.	yr.	To mo.	yr.	Full Time	Part Time	Fields of Study and Special Courses	Number of Hours Completed	Diploma or Degree	Grade Point Average
High School	Lincoln Sr. High Bailey Pike + Rte. 63 Aurora, IL 60506	9	88	6	92	✓	—	College Prep.	—	Diploma	3.8 (4 pt. scale)
College	Aurora Comm. College 3000 Crestline Aurora, IL 60504	9	92	5	94	✓	—	major: Fashion minor: Marketing	—	A.A.	3.5 (4 pt. scale)
Other	Aurora Univ. Extension 700 Galena Ave. Aurora, IL 60506	7	94	8	94	—	✓	Photography	—	Certificate of Completion	Pass (Pass/Fail)
Other	Saltaire Textile Institute P.O. Box 9091 Aurora, IL 60507	7	94	2	95	✓	—	Textile Design + Fabrication	—	Certificate of Achievement	3.8 (4 pt. scale)
GED	Date Received: —							Location: —			

Circle the highest grade completed: 1 2 3 4 5 6 7 8 9 10 11 12 13 (14) 15 16 16+

Today most job applications do not ask about education below the high school level. Such information could be important, however, for those who have not completed high school. Job seekers in this position may include entries for primary and/or junior high school in the rows marked Other. They should also circle the appropriate completion level at the bottom of the chart.

Education and Training Statement

Now that you have compiled your education and training data, you can develop a statement from it for use in interviews. You should be prepared to explain how your education and training relate to the position you want. Here is an example: "My interest in nursing started when I took a first aid course in high school. After graduating, I took a job as a nurse's aide. I was trained to take vital signs and do patient care. When I decided to become a practical nurse, I worked and trained at Regency Medical Center. Now I have my degree, and I think my training can be useful at the Vanderlee Clinic." Now try your own statement.

MY EDUCATION AND TRAINING STATEMENT

_____

_____

_____

_____

_____

_____

Job-Related Personal Information

Employers want to know everything about you that relates to their job opening. On the DataTrakt pages titled Job-Related Personal Information, you will record a wide range of relevant data. You will use this data throughout your job search.

Position Desired

As stated earlier, you should know what job you want and can do well before you specify the position you desire. This bit of data will provide the direction for your job search. When you know what you want to do, print the title of that job in your DataTrakt.

Sometimes your first choice won't be available. Is there a second job that you feel qualified for and are willing to accept? If so, list this job as your second choice.

Salary Desired

If you know what salary you want and it is a reasonable sum, record your desired salary. Otherwise, leave the space blank for now. You will read more about this subject in Chapter 3. That information may affect your decision about the figure you want to use, if any.

Availability

Think about when you will be available to start work. (Do not start a new job one week if you plan to take a trip or vacation the next week.) Decide what hours and days you will be available for regular work. Consider your life-style, family, and ability to adjust to a new schedule. Are you really willing to work weekends, overtime, and holidays? Many people say this until the time comes to show up for work. Don't say you are willing if you're really not. The best approach is to be as flexible as possible. You can always refuse a job offer later. Print in your DataTrakt the date, hours, and days that you will be available. Also, indicate your willingness or unwillingness to relocate.

Certification, Registration, and Licenses

Information about certification, registration, and licenses is required on some applications. This is to determine whether or not you are qualified to practice a certain occupation. Electricians, medical technicians, nurses, and teachers are examples of workers who are certified. If you have a professional certification, registration, or license, print that information in your DataTrakt. If not, put a dash in the space.

Some applications require your driver's license number. Some also ask what type of driver's license you have (such as operator or chauffeur, truck driver or motorcyclist). Print in your DataTrakt the information about your driver's license.

Professional Organizations

Professional organizations are established to promote the interests of certain vocational fields. Professional organizations may be either local, state, national, or international. Examples include state teachers' associations, the American Federation of Service Managers, the National Association of Computer Programmers, and the National Association of Broadcasters—to name a few.

In your DataTrakt, print the names of any professional organizations to which you belong. Also, print other relevant data, such as your title (if you have one) or membership number. Put dashes in these spaces if you do not belong to any organizations.

Interests and Hobbies

An interest is a personal feeling, concern, or curiosity about something. A hobby is similar to an interest. It is something you like to do or study in your spare time.

You may have interests or hobbies related to the job you are seeking. Employers recognize that this will make you like your work more. Thus, you will probably perform better and stay on the job longer than other applicants. This helps make you the right person for the job.

If you have taken the time to find out what job you really want, you probably have interests and hobbies related to this type of work. If so, list these interests and hobbies in your DataTrakt.

Now read the following examples of interest and hobby statements made by other job seekers.

- "When I was in school, I took all the bookkeeping, accounting, and math courses I could. Numbers fascinate me. I know I would enjoy being a bookkeeper with this firm."

- "I've been interested in music all my life. I started piano lessons when I was six. Later I learned brass, percussion, and guitar. I compose and arrange my own songs. I've taught piano and guitar privately for four years. I would be a dedicated salesperson in your music store because I believe people should make their own music."

- "I love flowers. My house is nearly a jungle of vines, buds, and bouquets. In the summer I have a large flower garden. I've taken courses in horticulture and floral arrangement from the free university. I'd truly enjoy working in your shop and greenhouse."

You should be prepared to make a similar statement in an interview. In the space below, write two simple statements about your interests and hobbies. Also, show how that interest or hobby connects to your job objective and supports your entry into a particular line of work. These statements might help convince an employer that you are the right person for the job.

INTERESTS AND HOBBIES

Statement: _____

_____

_____

_____

Connection: _____

_____

INTERESTS AND HOBBIES

Statement: _____

_____

_____

_____

Connection: _____

_____

Successes and Achievements

For some strange reason, most people forget to discuss their personal, work, and social successes during a job interview. They justify this omission any number of ways: "I don't want to toot my own horn." "It sounds too much like bragging." "They should like me for what I am."

The Work Book response to these people is simple: How will employers get this important information about you unless you tell them? Telling the facts about your successes is good strategy. You wouldn't want another applicant to talk about his or her successes and beat you out of a job, would you?

"What's a success?" you ask. It could be that you taught yourself to be a mechanic, that you have always done everything to perfection, or that you starred in a local theatrical production. Anything that you feel is a success is one. In your DataTrakt list your life, work, and educational successes.

Now, from the successes listed in your DataTrakt, pick four that might show employers that you're better qualified than other applicants. Then use the forms on the following page to write statements that connect those successes to employer expectations. If you're on a "success roll," use a separate sheet of paper to identify more of your successes.

SUCCESSES AND ACHIEVEMENTS

Statement: _____

_____

_____

_____

Connection: _____

_____

SUCCESSES AND ACHIEVEMENTS

Statement: _____

_____

_____

_____

Connection: _____

_____

SUCCESSES AND ACHIEVEMENTS

Statement: _____

_____

_____

_____

Connection: _____

_____

SUCCESSES AND ACHIEVEMENTS

Statement: _____

_____

_____

_____

Connection: _____

_____

Transferable Skills and Self-Management Skills

Your final exercise in this section is to review your lists of transferable skills and self-management skills from Chapter 1. Take what you consider to be your top ten entries from each list, and compare them with the type of work you are seeking. If you believe they match up well with the types of skills needed to do the job, list them in the Transferable Skills and Self-Management Skills sections of your DataTrakt booklet. If your skills don't match up, go back through each list to identify other skills you have that do match.

References

A reference is a person who will speak about your good qualities to an employer. The people you choose as references should know something about your work skills, personality traits, education, life experiences, and transferable skills. If you want your references to reinforce your employment value, they need to know about you and be willing to give a positive recommendation.

You might be thinking, "Employers don't check references, do they?" You bet they do if they're planning to stay in business. Choosing your references and keeping track of information about them is an important part of your job search.

There are two basic kinds of references—employer and personal. In effect, you selected your employer references when you listed your supervisor or a substitute back in the Work Experience section of your DataTrakt. Those are the people a potential employer will contact first. Personal references include everyone else.

Since you want every reference to be positive, you should choose your personal references with care. You'll need about four. Select people who know your work or character—instructors, good friends, neighbors, co-workers, and ministers, for example. Contact them to ask if they will agree to be your reference and if they are willing to respond to both phone and written inquiries.

Make sure they know the type of work you are seeking. Mention briefly what you would like them to say about you. Make sure they are comfortable with your summation of your skills. Never ask a reference to "bend the truth."

Send each reference some supportive materials. These might include JIST cards (which you will learn about in Chapter 4) and possibly even resumes (Chapter 8). Explain that they can use these items when asked to speak on your behalf. Whatever you supply, make sure it includes your job objective.

Fill out the personal reference forms in your DataTrakt while you are talking with your references. Make sure you have all of the necessary information and that you have spelled their names correctly.

A Work in Progress

Congratulations—your DataTrakt is now three-fourths complete! It is already a significant tool for your job search. It contains most of the basic information that employers will want to know about you. And thanks to its convenient size, you now have a pocket or purse full of personal data.

Carry your DataTrakt with you throughout your job search. Do not rely on memory, which can fail you. Your DataTrakt has all of the dates, telephone numbers, names, and addresses that employers could require. It will give you the information and the confidence you need to meet employers' basic expectations.

CHAPTER THREE

Applications

Screening Yourself into the Running

The application is the paper tool most familiar to job seekers. It contains questions about a job seeker's personal and work-related data. For the employer, an application is a screening device, a way to eliminate undesirable applicants from consideration. It is also the basis for most interview questions. Finally, when a person is hired, the application becomes part of his or her employee record.

In this chapter you will learn how to produce a near-perfect applications. You will also learn how to power up an application so that it screens you into, not out of, the running for an interview. This is especially important since only 1 percent of applications completed actually lead to an interview!

This chapter should help you make a good first impression with your applications. How? By making those applications meet the major expectations of employers:

- *Appearance.* Your applications will be neat, complete, and accurate.

- *Dependability.* Applications contain many entries that you can use to showcase your dependability—places where you can cite previous responsibilities you've been given or good attendance.

- *Skills.* Most applications ask if you possess certain skills or give you an opportunity to list the skills you have.

Before You Even Start

During your job search you will probably fill out many applications. To help ensure that yours will be among the best that each employer sees, carefully read and work through the exercises that follow. As you do, remember that the way you present your information is as important as its content.

Being Prepared

Be prepared to fill out an application whenever you apply for a job. Bring the following:

- *Pen.* A fine-tip pen with blue or black ink (preferably erasable) would be the best choice for filling out applications.

- *DataTrakt booklet.* Once completed, your personal DataTrakt should provide you with all the information you need for an application.

- *Pocket dictionary.* Use this to check the spelling of any word you are unsure of.

- *White out.* Carry this with you to correct any mistakes or remove any smudges you make while filling out applications.

- *JIST cards.* Carry a small packet of these, enough to attach to applications you fill out and to leave with employers who interview you.

- *Resumes.* As with JIST cards, carry a small packet—enough to attach to applications and leave with interviewers.

- *Small note pad.* Use this to keep notes on applications and interviews.

- *Pencils and an eraser.* Should you have to take a test as part of the application process, these will likely be provided. Still, your planning and forethought in bringing your own could impress a potential employer.

Following Instructions

Be sure to read all directions *before* writing any data on an application. Many applications begin with general instructions, such as "Print in ink" or "To be handprinted in ink or typewritten." Separate instructions may tell you how to present information for each section or item. Other instructions may tell you not to put any data in a certain space.

Following instructions is important. Employers want to hire people who can follow instructions on the job. Employers will not have a high regard for your dependability and skill if you cannot follow instructions on an application.

Using Dashes

Some application questions will not apply to you. Make a short dash (—) after each of these questions. The dash is a simple, attractive way to tell employers that you have read the question, but that it does not apply to you.

Leaving Blank Spaces

It is sometimes better to leave a blank space on your application than to write information that could hurt your chances of getting a job. An application will not get you a job. It can, however, keep you from being considered for one. If an honest answer to an application question is negative or could easily be misunderstood, leave that item blank. Do not even make a dash in the space. You can explain the blank in an interview, if necessary. In this way your failure to respond will not automatically be used to screen you out of a job for which you might otherwise qualify.

Expect employers to question you about blank spaces. Be prepared to answer their questions. If a blank space is not discussed in the course of an interview, be sure to mention it after you are offered a job. This will prevent you from being fired later for withholding information.

An alternative to leaving a space blank is to write, "Will explain in interview." Decide for yourself which way is better for you.

Powering Up Your Application

You want to make sure that your application is one that will lead to an interview. Consider the "rules of thumb" listed below as you work your way through this chapter. They will help you produce the most persuasive, powerful application possible.

- *Realize that applications are "closed systems."* There's only so much space in each section and only so much room on each application to show employers how you will meet their expectations. This means that you must make every word count. To ensure that you are using your space wisely, compare your information with the employer's expectations. If your information meets any one of those expectations, it's probably a good use of space.

- *Follow the rules—until they stop you from showing employers your value.* Most applications gather only basic information, and they don't do that very well. If you need to expand on information or counter a problem area, attach an extra sheet of paper or an index card. It's even okay to write in the margins and above or below words—if you do it neatly.

- *Do not use "lazy" responses.* Many people try to escape the work of completing an application by writing, "See attached resume." Others, not wanting to write out the same information twice, simply state, "Same" or "See above." Neither of these tactics contributes to a persuasive, powerful application.

- *Counterbalance negative situations with positive information.* Never write negative information. If you choose to enter information that might be seen as negative (disabilities, reasons for leaving your last job, etc.), you must also show the employer that you are able and willing to do everything necessary to get the job and do it well. You always have at least five options for problem sections:

1. Lie and try to get away with it. This is *not* advisable and is unfair to the employer.
2. Use a dash (—) for problem sections, and plan on discussing the topic during an interview.
3. Tell the truth and present a counterbalancing statement on the form.
4. Print, "Will discuss in interview." This may or may not help you.
5. Leave the section blank and plan on discussing it during an interview.

Only you can decide which of these options is the right one for you. If you are not sure about what to do, discuss the matter with your teacher or counselor.

- ***Read the application front and back before beginning to fill it out.*** Many applications have a section on the last page that begins with the statement, "Do not write below this line." The information in this section often tells you how the employer will evaluate the application. This can give you clues about how you should answer certain questions.

- ***Redo poorly done applications, if possible.*** Many job applicants wish they could go back and redo applications they completed poorly. If you find yourself in this situation, return to the employer. Explain that you need to upgrade your information and would like a new application to complete. You want only good information in your file.

Standard Entries

Over the last decade or two, the trend has been to simplify job applications. Employers have dispensed with much of the information they used to request. They have removed items relating to age, marital status, health, disabilities, and ethnic origins. They have done so to conform to a variety of federal antidiscrimination statutes.

This is not to say that employers no longer need such data. They do and may ask for it, but only *after* a person has been hired. Employers need to know age for pension and social security purposes. They need to know about marital status for health and other insurance plans. They may even need to know ethnic and/or racial background to meet work force diversity goals. But again, this is after hiring or an offer of employment.

Before that point, while screening job applicants, employers must observe the strict guidelines that have "emptied out" today's application forms. Employers cannot legally ask applicants to provide certain kinds of information. We will discuss these "forbidden" areas and what you should do if asked about them later in the chapter. But first, we'll consider those items that regularly—and legally—appear on most job applications. They fall into five basic categories:

1. Identification
   - Name
   - Social security number
   - Address
   - Telephone number
   - Physical traits
   - Age
   - Citizenship
   - Eligibility to work
   - Emergency information

2. Employment Objectives
   - Position desired
   - Salary desired
   - Availability
   - Transportation

3. Education

4. Experience
   - Work experience
   - Military experience
   - Volunteer activities
   - Certification, registration, and licenses
   - Professional organizations
   - Clubs and organizations
   - Hobbies and interests
   - Other skills

5. References

To learn how to fill out an application, follow the instructions for each exercise in this chapter. Use a pencil so that you can make corrections, and print your data neatly. Above all, use your DataTrakt. It will help you complete the exercises correctly and easily.

Name

You may need to give your name many times on a basic application. The way you are asked to list your name may be different each time. Be sure to read the instructions before listing even this most familiar data.

You will need to sign most applications. Your signature is your name as you normally write it when signing checks and legal papers. You should carefully read and verify all statements on the application before signing it.

Never list a nickname on your job-search tools unless there is a special blank for it. You want to show employers that you are businesslike. Use your complete, legal name.

The blanks below are typical of the kinds you will find on applications. Print your name according to the instructions provided.

Print Name

_____

(Last)   (First)   (Middle Initial)

Name

_____

First   Middle   Last

Print: Last Name, First Name, Middle Initial

APPLICANT'S SIGNATURE _____

Print Name

(Last)

(First)

(Middle)

Social Security Number

Be sure to print your social security number so that it is readable and correct. Many companies use their employees' social security numbers in filing and computer systems. An error in your social security number could cause problems with your payments, benefits, taxes, retirement, and unemployment account.

Your social security number should be printed correctly on your DataTrakt. Verify this: check your DataTrakt against your social security card. Be sure the number is clearly divided into its three parts, and check each individually for accuracy. Then enter your number below.

Social Security No. (SSN)			

Address

All applications ask for your current address. Some also ask for your previous address. Others distinguish between temporary and permanent residences. In any of these cases, you may need to state how long you lived or have lived at the address. You already have this information in your DataTrakt. Rather than spending time remembering house numbers, zip codes, and dates, put your effort into transferring your data correctly to your application.

Before you list your address, read the instructions. Then be sure to put all your data in the correct spaces. If the application does not ask for a certain order, list your address as follows: street address; rural route, or box number; city, state, and zip code.

Address   *1104 N. 4th St., Terre Haute, IN 47807*

Consider how you will answer when asked how long you have lived at a certain address. This information will give employers an impression of stability. Of course, you want all impressions to be favorable. If you have lived at your current address for five years or more, you may choose to put a dash in the blank for previous address. If you have lived at your current address for a short time (less than two years), the length of time at your previous address may offset this.

Following are examples of address sections commonly found on applications. Print your data in the correct spaces.

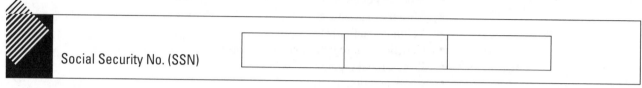

ADDRESS			
No.	Street	City/State	Zip

Present Address	Years at Location

Home Address (#, Street)	City	State	Zip

Previous Address (if less than 2 years at current address)

Telephone Number

Many employers prefer to contact applicants by telephone rather than by mail. This lets employers receive the applicants' responses right away. Therefore, your telephone number could be as important in getting you employed as any other data on your application.

List a phone number that is likely to be answered during the day. If no one will be answering the phone, or if you do not have a phone, list the number of someone who can accept messages for you. This person should be a reliable friend or relative. Choose someone who will be polite, take your messages accurately, and get word to you quickly. And be sure to tell him or her that potential employers might be calling.

To ensure employers will be able to reach you, follow these suggestions before listing your phone number on an application. Neatly print your complete, correct number. Begin with your area code. Then list the number. Do not guess! Many people have trouble remembering their own numbers since they seldom call home. Refer to your DataTrakt. Note the following examples of complete, correctly written telephone numbers.

Telephone Number (319)555-0228   Telephone Number 319-555-0228

Many businesses, schools, and large offices have switchboard-extension systems. If your phone is an extension unit, you will need to include your extension number. See the examples below.

Telephone Number (812)555-0921, Ext.21   Telephone Number 812-555-0921 (x21)

It is always a good idea to list two phone numbers. If the first number goes unanswered or is busy, employers can try the second number. Without a second number, they might call the next applicant on their list. Therefore, list your home number and work number, or the number of a reliable friend. Note that most applications do not have separate blanks for two numbers. The examples below show how you might fit them in.

Telephone Number (611)555-1116/555-7112   Telephone Number (611) 555-1116 (611) 555-7112

Having a phone is a positive point for potential employees. If you have a phone, employers know they can contact you for overtime work or in an emergency. Also, having a telephone implies a certain amount of stability.

Print your complete, correct telephone number(s) in the spaces provided. If you have no numbers to write, put dashes above the lines.

Telephone Number _____   Telephone Number _____

Physical Traits

Few jobs require applicants to have particular physical traits. However, those that do (like police officer and fire fighter) usually request information on height and weight.

When listing your physical features on an application, print the correct and most current information. Use the spaces below to practice. (Give your height using symbols as well as words for units of measurement.)

Height _____   Height _____ ft. _____ in.

Weight _____   Weight _____ lbs.

Age

If you are a young job seeker, you will be asked to prove your age—or at least your age level—before an employer will consider hiring you. The employer's primary concern here is to determine if you are old enough to work without restriction. If you are under 18, you may be subject to limits on the kind of work you can do, when, and for how many hours each week. You will also probably need a valid work permit from the state.

These issues are usually dealt with briefly, using entries like those below. Answer as you would on a job application.

Are you under the age of 18?   ☐ Yes   If yes, can you furnish a valid work permit?   ☐ Yes
                                ☐ No   ☐ No

Citizenship

Applications often include a question about citizenship. You must indicate whether or not you are a citizen of the United States. Noncitizens are usually asked to list their visa number and type. If you are not a U.S. citizen, but have applied for citizenship, give the date on which you applied. Note the following examples.

U.S. Citizen   ☑ Yes ☐ No   U.S. Citizen   ☐ Yes ☑ No
If no, list visa number and type: If no, list visa number and type:

Number_____—_____   Number__317206D__
Type_____—_____   Type_____7-12-93_____

Now, in the space below, list your citizenship data.

Are you a U.S. citizen?   If no, visa number and type:

☐ Yes   ☐ No   Number _____   Type _____

Eligibility to Work

Remember, one of the first things you will be asked to do as a new employee is prove your eligibility to work in the United States. This fulfills a legal requirement that employers must meet.

If a new employee cannot provide the documents to prove his or her status, employment can be refused—an awkward, wasteful situation for all concerned. Therefore, some employers try to anticipate a potential employee's answer by questioning on a job application. The inquiry is usually made in the simplest form possible:

If hired, can you present evidence of your legal right to work   ☑ Yes
in the United States?   ☐ No

"Evidence" consists of one or more documents like these: a passport, a driver's license, a green card, a social security card, or a birth certificate. By the time you have started filling out job applications, you should have obtained the documents you will use to meet this requirement.

Emergency Information

Many applications ask for the name and address of someone to contact in an emergency. There are two reasons why you should answer these questions. The first reason is obvious—to be sure your family will be notified. The second reason is to show your stability. Employers might think you are a "drifter" (and thus unreliable) if you do not list the name of someone who would be concerned about you.

You may list a close friend if no relatives live nearby. Otherwise, list a relative. Print your data in the form below.

In case of an emergency, contact:

Name _____ Relationship _____

Address _____ Phone _____

Position Desired

Most applications ask you to state the position you desire. If you respond, "Any job," you cannot hope to make a good impression. All the other information on your application will probably not indicate an ability to do just "any job." It will show your skills, accomplishments, and experiences gained from previous jobs. It will suggest at least a direction if not an outright job objective.

Thus, you will be more appreciated and respected by employers if you know which job you want. But how do you find out the correct title to use? You will gradually accumulate this information throughout your job-search experience. Position titles will be suggested by friends and relatives who are already on the job in places that interest you. They will come from employers you speak with by phone while looking for job leads. They will come from your teachers or counselors. They may even come from want ads or personnel departments. Over time you will learn enough to describe the kind of position you want.

Ideally, that description will be specific but also flexible. That way you can screen yourself into a range of employer possibilities. But how do you achieve these opposite goals? By stating your desired position in a way that keeps open several options. First, you list the title of the job you want. Then you add titles of similar or related positions. Note the following examples.

Position Desired **WAREHOUSE WORKER**
(SHIPPING CLERK, DRIVER)

Position Desired **WAREHOUSE WORKER**
(OR SIMILAR POSITION)

By showing employers that you have a specific goal but are open to options, you increase your chances of being employed. Print the titles of your desired positions in each of the following sample forms.

Position(s) applied for _____

Type of Work Desired (check one):

Sales _____   Office _____   Warehouse _____   Maintenance _____

Other (specify): _____

Salary Desired

Applications commonly provide space for you to specify your desired salary. This subject can pose a problem if you have not researched the job market. You do not want to undersell yourself. Nor do you want to price yourself out of the market with a wild guess. You can research the job market by following these suggestions:

- Read want ads that list salaries for similar positions.

- Call your local employment office, and ask the salary range for your type of job.

- Talk with people who do the kind of work you want.

You may list a specific salary, a high-low range, or leave the space blank. However, the best response is to print, "Open." This is a positive word. It will not commit you to a figure either too low or too high.

Where it occurs, the salary item on an application usually consists of a single blank. This leaves it up to you to decide the form of your answer. Should you choose to enter a dollar amount or a range, be sure to specify a rate or pay period. You have five choices: hourly, weekly, biweekly (every two weeks), monthly, or annually. Here are some examples.

Salary expected: $ _5.50_ per _HR._   Salary expected: $ _200_ per _WEEK_

Salary Requirements _$18,000 — $20,000 PER YEAR_

SALARY DESIRED _$1200 PER MONTH_   SALARY DESIRED _$1200/MO._

Most salaries quoted to you will be framed in hourly or annual terms. Want ads frequently use the monthly form. You should know, however, what your ideal salary or wages work out to in each form so that you can judge and discuss any offer intelligently. Practice how you will state your salary requirements on an application.

Salary Desired _____   SALARY _____

Availability

Questions about when you will be available for work are often included on applications. This data helps employers make schedules that satisfy everyone.

You will almost certainly be asked to state the date that you can start work. The day you give should fit your schedule. Do not start a job one week and expect to take a vacation the next. Do not begin a job one day if you intend to keep a dental appointment the next.

You may also be asked to indicate the kind of work you want in terms of overall hours. The usual choices offered are full-time, part-time, and temporary or seasonal employment.

Finally, you will most likely be asked to list the days and hours you will be available for work. The best responses here are "All shifts" and "All hours." This shows your flexibility. Many jobs consist of a Monday-to-Friday workweek with possible overtime on weekends. Some jobs regularly include weekend work. On other jobs the work schedules change every week or month. The more flexible you are, the greater your chances of being interviewed and hired. If your life-style, family, or other factors limit you to a certain shift, you can refuse job offers for other shifts. If an employer has already determined that you are the right person for the job, you might be changed to your desired shift.

You should already have your availability data recorded in your DataTrakt. Refer to the Job-Related Personal Information section, and answer the following questions.

I am seeking: □ full-time work   Date available: _____
              □ part-time work
              □ seasonal work

Times available: Mon.   Tues.   Wed.   Thurs.   Fri.   Sat.   Sun.

From   _____   _____   _____   _____   _____   _____   _____

To   _____   _____   _____   _____   _____   _____   _____

Transportation

Some application questions are concerned with transportation. Such questions are most common when a job involves driving—either a company vehicle or your own. In such cases, an employer will usually ask for information about your driver's license.

Why? Put yourself in the employer's place. If you were going to trust an applicant with a delivery truck, wouldn't you want to be sure he or she could drive that type of vehicle? (A truck is a very costly piece of equipment.) If an applicant were going to be driving *any* kind of vehicle on business, wouldn't you want to know about his or her driving record? (Insurance is an extremely costly business expense and gets more expensive with increased claims.) Motor vehicle records can shed light on both of these areas.

Once again, refer to the Job-Related Personal Information section of your DataTrakt booklet. Then print your data in the forms below.

Driver's License No. _____   Type _____   Expiration _____

Do you have a valid Motor Vehicle Operator's License?   □ Yes   □ No

If yes, specify: State _____   Lic. # _____   Exp. date _____

Education

All applications ask about your educational history. In fact, most require quite a bit of information in this section. You will be able to give complete and accurate information by using your DataTrakt. Its Education and Training chart is typical of education sections on most applications.

You should include the full names and addresses of all schools in the appropriately labeled spaces. List military training and volunteer training in this section as well if they are not asked for elsewhere on an application.

You should be able to account for all the time you spent in school and training. This information could be important in explaining gaps in your job history. List the number of hours completed for any unfinished course of study or training. For instance, if you left high school after your third year, list the number of completed semester hours or semesters. This will help offset your lack of a diploma. Otherwise, you would leave this space blank and discuss it during an interview.

Be sure to list your GED (General Education Diploma) if you have one. Some applications will not ask for this information specifically. In such a case, print the data about your GED in either the High School or Other blanks or their equivalents. Here are two examples based on your DataTrakt booklet of how to include your GED.

School	Name of School and Complete Address	From		To		Full Time	Part Time	Fields of Study and Special Courses	Number of Hours Completed	Diploma or Degree	Grade Point Average
		mo.	yr.	mo.	yr.						
Other	Filmore Ed. Ctr. 1100 N. Main St. Carlin, CA 95872	8	90	4	91	—	✓	GED	—	Diploma	—

School	Name of School and Complete Address	From		To		Full Time	Part Time	Fields of Study and Special Courses	Number of Hours Completed	Diploma or Degree	Grade Point Average
		mo.	yr.	mo.	yr.						
GED	Filmore Ed. Ctr. 1100 N. Main St. Carlin, CA 95872	8	90	4	91	—	✓	General	—	Diploma	—

Some applications ask you to show the highest grade you completed. As with all your data, be accurate and neat. If you have a GED, refer to it here. Note the following examples.

What is the highest grade you have completed? GED

Circle the highest grade completed:
1   2   3   4   5   6   7   8   9   10   11   (12)   13   14   15   16   16+

If you have not had much education or training, you may choose to skip the education section of an application. Knowing what you want to do and being able to do it well are the important things. If you have these qualities, you can convince an employer during the interview that you are the right person for the job.

Print your education and training data in the following form as you would on an application. This exercise will be easy if you consult your DataTrakt.

School (Name and Address)	Dates	Course/ Major	Type Degree/ Certificate	Graduated
High School	From To			☐ Yes ☐ No
Bus./Tech./Voc. School	From To			☐ Yes ☐ No
Jr. College/College	From To			☐ Yes ☐ No
Other	From To			☐ Yes ☐ No

Work Experience

On almost every job application, work experience requires more data than any other section. Generally employers regard this as the most important part of an application.

You should be well prepared to list your work history. Your DataTrakt has all the work experience data needed to fill out an application. Make sure your DataTrakt is complete. Use it when you list your work experience on an application.

Refer to your DataTrakt now. Use it to complete the following work experience forms. List the data for your most recent job *first*. List your next most recent job in the second form, and so on. Notice that each form is different. Print your data according to the instructions in each. If you have no work experience, leave the forms blank. You should be prepared to offset this during an interview.

WORK HISTORY

	Employer	Job Duties	Employment Dates From	Employment Dates To	Last Pay Rate	Reason for leaving
Present or Most Recent Job	Co. Name _____ Address _____ City/State/Zip _____ Phone #( ) _____ Supervisor Name _____					

EMPLOYMENT HISTORY

COMPANY NAME AND ADDRESS	DATES MO.	DATES YR.	POSITION DATA		REASONS FOR LEAVING
COMPANY	F R O M		TITLE	SUPERVISOR	
ADDRESS					
CITY/STATE/ZIP	T O		RATE OF PAY	PHONE NUMBER ( ) -	

WORK EXPERIENCE

DATE From	DATE To	SALARY Starting	SALARY Leaving	EMPLOYER AND ADDRESS	POSITION TITLE	REASON FOR LEAVING
Mo. Yr.	Mo. Yr.	$ Per	$ Per	Employer _____ No. & St. _____ City & State – ZIP Ph. ( )		

WORK HISTORY

MOST RECENT EMPLOYER	ADDRESS	PHONE
DATE STARTED Starting Salary $ per	STARTING POSITION	
DATE LEFT Ending Salary $ per	LEAVING POSITION	
NAME AND TITLE OF SUPERVISOR		
DESCRIPTION OF DUTIES	REASON FOR LEAVING	

Military Experience

Most applications ask for data about military experience. The amount of information requested can range from a few lines to a detailed history.

If you were honorably discharged, you should accurately list all the data required. Consult your DataTrakt. If you received something less than an honorable discharge, leave this section blank. In this case, be prepared to discuss your military background in an interview. Be ready to give reasonable, positive answers. Put a dash in each blank if you were never in the service. Try your hand at filling out these entries:

Did you serve in the military? _____ If so, what branch? _____

Dates of induction/discharge _____ / Rank attained _____

Service-related skills applicable to the position you are seeking

_____

_____

_____

If you were honorably discharged, you are eligible for Veteran Preference Points. These points help you get certain government jobs. Keep this in mind as you begin your job search. To be credited with these points, you may need to obtain special forms. Ask your local Veterans Administration office for details. Also, contact the VA if you are a Vietnam veteran and are having trouble finding work. Many VA offices have job placement programs and offer career counseling.

Volunteer Experience

List all of your volunteer experience on applications. Volunteer experience is a type of work experience and just as important. Volunteer activities usually require certain duties, responsibilities, and training. Information about these activities will meet two of the employer's main expectations—dependability and skill. This data may also cover a potential job gap.

Many applications have special sections for data about your volunteer experience. Others do not. If there is no special section, list your volunteer activities in the work experience section.

Certification, Registration, and Licenses

Some applications provide space to list the professional and legal documents required for certain certifications. These documents are necessary in fields such as medicine, law, engineering, teaching, aviation, and accounting. If you have any professional certifications, registrations, or licenses, practice entering them on the form below. Consult your DataTrakt. Put a dash in each space that does not pertain to you.

Are you certified, registered, or licensed in any profession? _____

If yes, give complete information, including number and expiration date.

_____

_____

Professional Organizations

Employers may be interested in the professional organizations to which you belong. Such a membership is especially important if the organization and job are directly related. However, membership in any professional organization supports your dependability and skill.

When listing your professional memberships, you should include any offices or titles you hold. Note the difference between these two entries:

NAT'L. ASSOC. OF BROADCASTERS   GRAPHIC ARTISTS FORUM, CHAIRPERSON

Now refer to your DataTrakt, and print your entries in the blank form provided. Place a dash in each space if you do not belong to any professional organizations. (Do not list social organizations or activities.)

List the professional organizations to which you belong.

_____   _____

Clubs and Organizations

Some applications ask about the clubs and nonprofessional organizations to which you belong. This information gives employers a more personal impression of you. Membership in a club or organization indicates an active person who can "get along" with other people. Being active and sociable are positive worker traits.

If you do not belong to any organizations and do not take part in activities outside of school or work, place a dash after such questions. It is also better to use a dash than to list membership in potentially controversial organizations, like political groups. Otherwise, list your clubs, organizations, activities, and titles, if you have any.

Read the examples below. Then list your own data in the form that follows.

List clubs and organizations to which you belong. _____

_____

List any relevant extracurricular activities. _____

_____

Hobbies and Interests

An employer may have a special interest in you if one of your hobbies closely relates to your desired job. This can save the employer time and money since you will need less training than other job seekers. You will also be more apt to stay with the job because it will be personally satisfying. Note the example below. The position desired by this applicant is electronics technician.

List your hobbies, interests, and leisure-time activities.

AS A "HAM" RADIO OPERATOR, I ENJOY DESIGNING AND BUILDING MY OWN EQUIPMENT. I DO EXTENSIVE READING IN TECHNICAL JOURNALS, CONCENTRATING ON INNOVATIVE COMPONENT ASSEMBLY TECHNIQUES.

Refer to your DataTrakt to determine which of your hobbies and interests relate to your desired position. List those that are most closely related in the first column of blanks below. In the second column, explain how each hobby relates to the position you want. Note that you will use only the data in the left-hand column on applications. You will use the information in the second column during interviews.

Hobbies	Relation to Work
_____	_____
_____	_____
_____	_____
_____	_____
_____	_____

Other Skills

Applications often ask for other skills, abilities, experience, and training related to your desired job. This section may reveal some of your best qualifications.

You have most likely listed all of your qualifications in your DataTrakt already. However, there may be some that you have not yet entered there. Perhaps they do not quite fit into any of the given categories. Remember, though, you cannot list too many. Consult your DataTrakt. Try to think of items you may have overlooked. Then print your entry for this typical application item:

Other skills, abilities, experience, or training related to the position:

_____

_____

_____

_____

References

Most applications ask for a brief list of personal references. Be sure you have your DataTrakt with you when you fill in these sections. Otherwise, it will be impossible for you to remember all of your reference information.

Practice using your DataTrakt and listing your personal references on the form below.

List three persons you have known for at least one year who are not relatives or former employers.

Name	Address	Phone	Occupation

Problem Items

Very early in this chapter, it was noted that today's job applications have been "emptied out" by antidiscrimination statutes. Just because it's illegal to ask certain questions on a job application, however, doesn't mean that you'll never find such questions there. Not all employers have gotten the message. (This is particularly true of small business owners who don't have personnel and legal departments to keep them up on the latest regulations.) And even those employers who have gotten the message may interpret it differently.

Still, you are not likely to find *many* application questions on such forbidden topics such as race, gender, marital status, and age. Why? Because of the very nature of a job application. A job application is a document. It's printed, and because of this, illegal items are easy to spot—and report, and eliminate. Violations are far more likely to occur in the give-and-take of an interview.

Today there seem to be only two major areas where employers have yet to decide what is and what is not allowed under the law on a job application. Those areas are criminal record and applicant health.

Criminal Record

Many applications ask if a job seeker has a criminal record. The way this question is phrased varies widely. Applicants are asked if they have ever been convicted of a crime, a crime other than a minor traffic violation, a felony, a felony or a misdemeanor, or any of a number of variations on each of these. In fact, the only legal form of inquiry is this one: Have you ever been convicted of a felony?

The key words in this question are *convicted* and *felony*. A person who has been "convicted" has been found guilty, unlike someone who has merely been "arrested" or "jailed." A person who has committed a "felony" has done something very seriously wrong, unlike someone who has merely committed a "misdemeanor."

If none of these terms applies to you, then answer no to this sort of question. If you have had some difficulties with the law but none that resulted in a felony conviction, then put a dash in the space provided. If you have been convicted of a felony, then leave the space blank and be prepared to discuss the subject in an interview. Discuss the matter as briefly as possible, and then move on to your positive qualifications at the first opportunity.

How will you deal with application questions on this difficult topic? Try your hand on the form below.

Have you ever been convicted of a felony? _____ If yes, explain.

_____

(*Note:* Conviction of a felony is not an automatic bar to employment.)

Consider the following points if you have been convicted of a felony.

- ***Bonding is sometimes required before an employer can hire someone convicted of a felony.*** Ask your local employment office for help if you need to be bonded.

- ***You would be wise not to seek a position related to your conviction.*** For instance, if you were convicted for selling drugs, do not apply for a nurse's aide position.

- ***You may have substantial gaps in your job history if you have spent time in jail.*** You should have attended to such gaps in the Work Experience section of your DataTrakt.

Applicant Health

The other application topic whose treatment is still evolving is applicant health. This area has been thrown into a state of confusion by the recent enactment of the Americans with Disabilities Act.

It used to be that on a job application you faced a whole battery of specific questions related to your health. These included whether you had certain diseases, took certain medications, or had any medical condition that an employer "ought to know about."

Today such inquiries are prohibited by the Americans with Disabilities Act (ADA). Employers can only legitimately ask if an applicant can perform specific, essential job tasks. For example, an employer can say, "This job would require you to lift boxes weighing up to 70 pounds. Can you do that?" Employers cannot ask applicants about disabilities that are not obvious, and applicants are not required to volunteer any information about such conditions. If an applicant does have a disability, the employer is required to provide "reasonable accommodation." An accommodation is any change in a job (when, where, or how it's done) that will allow a disabled person to do it.

One word of caution to all job applicants, however. The ADA does *not* apply to businesses with fewer than 15 employees. If you are seeking a job with such an employer, you may find yourself asked health-related questions on an application. What do you do? Just remember the standard DataTrakt rule: never write anything negative in your DataTrakt—or on an application. If you don't have the medical conditions or won't be kept from doing the job by them, then indicate that your health is excellent and that you have no health limitations. If there is a problem, then leave the entries blank and be prepared to discuss the situation in an interview.

Apply Yourself

Applications are the only job-search tool used by the average job seeker. The typical job seeker goes to a company, asks for an application, tries to fill it out from memory, and then waits for the employer's call. An active (but still average) job seeker will use this same approach but much more often. The approach works, but it does not work very well. Since only one tool is used, success depends greatly on how well the tool has been made. In this situation, the only other factor determining success is luck.

Having completed this chapter, you will do better at filling out applications than other job seekers. This means that you will likely get more interviews than average. Your application will provide a positive view of who you are relative to the job you want. It will meet each of the employer's major expectations. Its appearance will be neat (type if your printing is messy) and professional. It will show your dependability by listing your past responsibilities. And, it will show your skills by listing your education and experience.

Your application will be a strong tool. It is, however, only one tool. You need to learn about other tools you can use in your job search. JIST cards, telephone contacts, resumes, and the all-important interviews are tools explained in the following chapters. Use applications well. But do not be like the average job seeker and limit yourself to applications alone.

Before learning about other job-search tools, make sure you have learned your lessons about applications. As an exercise, try filling out the application that begins on the next page. During your job search, you can expect to see applications requiring different degrees of detail. Some are simpler than this sample, some more complex. Still, your work in this exercise will prepare you for most applications. Refer to your DataTrakt as you do the exercise. Use a pen with either black or blue ink. Take care to transfer your data neatly, without mistakes. Print your information unless instructed to do otherwise. Read and follow all instructions.

FLAGSTAR

APPLICATION FOR EMPLOYMENT

Indicate the Flagstar Company for which you are applying:

UNIT STAMP	Denny's ☐ EL POLLO LOCO ☐
Flagstar Companies, Inc. is an Equal Opportunity Employer	Hardee's ☐ Quincy's ☐

PLEASE PRINT CLEARLY, COMPLETE ALL ITEMS

PERSONAL INFORMATION: Date: _____   Social Security Number: _____

Name:_____ _____
        Last   First   Middle   Phone #

Present Address:_____
                Street   City   State   Zip

Previous Address:_____
                Street   City   State   Zip

Age (check one)   ☐ Under 16   ☐ 16 or 17   ☐ 18 or over
(If under 18 years of age a work permit or certificate may be required as a condition of employment.)

Have you ever worked for a company of Flagstar Companies, Inc. before?   ☐ Yes   ☐ No

If yes, when? _____
            From   To   Where   Division

How did you learn of our organization? ☐ Walk-In ☐ Newspaper   ☐ School   ☐ Referral   ☐ Agency   ☐ Other _____

EMPLOYMENT DESIRED: **Days & Hours available to work:**

Position:_____

Salary requirements:_____

Date you can start:_____

Have you ever applied to this company before? ☐ Yes ☐ No

If yes,_____ _____
        When   Where

☐ Check here if available any hours.

If restrictions, indicate available hours below.

	Mon	Tue	Wed	Thu	Fri	Sat	Sun
From							
To							

EDUCATION	Name and Location	Course of Study	Years Completed	Graduated	Degree Received
High School				Yes ☐ No ☐	
College				Yes ☐ No ☐	
Business, Trade Other				Yes ☐ No ☐	

REFERENCES: Give below the names of three persons not related to you, whom you have known at least one year.

Name	Phone	Address	Business	Years Known

REORDER NO. 1189   SFS - 001   (REV. 6/93)

GENERAL INFORMATION

What do you think are the most important factors in working in a Food-Service facility? _____

_____

_____

Have you ever been convicted of a felony within the past seven years?   Yes ☐   No ☐
(If yes, explain number of convictions, nature of offense (s) leading to each conviction, how recently such offense (s) was/were committed, sentence (s) for each conviction, and type of rehabilitation for each conviction.) _____

_____

_____

A conviction record is not an automatic bar to employment

FORMER EMPLOYERS:	List below last three employers, starting with your present or most recent employer. May we contact your former employers? Yes ☐ No ☐

Employer No. 1 (present or most recent)		Address		Phone Number
Employed (Month & Year) From To	Rate of Pay Start Final	Supervisor & Title		Avg./Hrs./Wk.
Your Job Title		Describe Your Duties		
Reason For Leaving				

Employer No. 2		Address		Phone Number
Employed (Month & Year) From To	Rate of Pay Start Final	Supervisor & Title		Avg./Hrs./Wk.
Your Job Title		Describe Your Duties		
Reason For Leaving				

Employer No. 3		Address		Phone Number
Employed (Month & Year) From To	Rate of Pay Start Final	Supervisor & Title		Avg./Hrs./Wk.
Your Job Title		Describe Your Duties		
Reason For Leaving				

PLEASE READ BEFORE SIGNING

I hereby verify that the information provided is true, complete, and accurate. I agree that the Company may investigate all of the statements made on this application form and that any misrepresentation or omission is cause for dismissal.

I understand that the Company may review references, credit files, and criminal records as part of the employment process.

I understand that no employee, manager, or other agent of the Company has the authority to enter into any agreement for employment for any specified period of time unless such an agreement is in writing and signed by the President of Flagstar Companies, Inc. I further understand that in the absence of such an agreement, employment can be terminated at the sole discretion of the company or employee at any time.

I understand that this application will remain active for 30 days.

Signature _____   Date _____

MARYLAND APPLICANTS ONLY:

Applicants and employees may not be required to submit to a polygraph or lie detector test as a condition of employment.
Signature _____   Date _____

Interviewed by _____   Date _____

Flagstar Companies, Inc., 203 East Main Street, Spartanburg, SC 29319

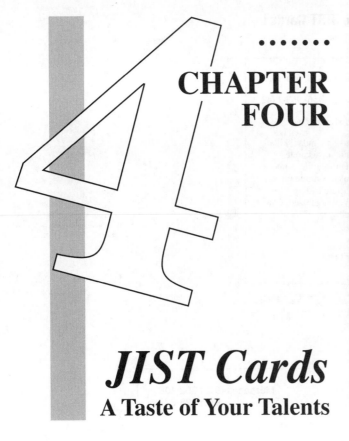

....

CHAPTER FOUR

JIST Cards
A Taste of Your Talents

JIST cards are one of the most powerful, unique, and practical job-search tools being used by job seekers today. The aim of a JIST card is to grab an employer's attention and show at a glance that your skills, abilities, and experiences match up with his or her expectations.

As you look at the sample JIST cards on the next page, notice how each is designed to meet an employer's expectations. Do you see how these cards will show an employer that you are a desirable candidate for an interview and the open position?

Aside from meeting an employer's expectations, your JIST card also helps you (and your interviewer) in the following ways:

* It effectively answers an interviewer's request for you to "tell me about yourself."

* You appear unique! No two cards look exactly alike or say the same thing.

* Your card quickly "hooks" the interest of an interviewer.

* How you present yourself on the phone (see Chapter 5) comes directly from the information on your JIST card.

* Your card shows employers that you know what you have to offer.

* During an interview, your card allows you to expand on the information it contains.

* Your confidence level goes up when you can complete and talk about your card.

* Your card shows that you are organized and possess important communication skills.

As you prepare your JIST card, you will be doing an exercise vital to your later training. By writing brief statements about your skills, you will be developing the vocabulary you need for speaking with employers. Pay attention! What you do here will affect every part of your job search.

Sample JIST Cards

John Chen   home (456) 654-1023

message (456) 963-1742

Vocational Objective: Accounting Clerk/Bookkeeper or related position

Capabilities: Nearly 2 years of related education and work, using similar skills. Graduate of bookkeeping program. Able to maintain accurate financial records; verify and post invoices, inventory, sales, time sheets, etc. Can summarize details, balance books, compile report statistics for planning and tax purposes. Can operate adding machine and use computerized spreadsheets. Well organized. Can troubleshoot problems and take instructions well.

Will work various shifts. Attendance record very good.

Honest, Accurate, Detail Minded, Eager Worker with Career Focus

---

Marsha Tharp   Messages (913) 962-1063
(913) 828-2871

Position Desired: Child Care

Skills: Nearly 16 years experience in child care. Have worked with mentally retarded and physically handicapped children. Can provide basic needs such as feeding and grooming. Can assist in recreational and instructional teaching. Enjoy working with others. Can work independently, react quickly in emergencies.

Willing to care for children evenings and weekends.

Patient   Sensitive   Hardworking

DANIEL GEVORKIAN   *(356) 543-8759*

(356) 547-3927

Field of Interest: General Office/Clerical

Knowledge/Skills: 2-plus years of actual work, education, and volunteer experiences using related skills. Graduate of vocational educational secretarial program (Honors). Can keyboard 50 wpm accurately using both electronic word processor and computer with word-processing software. Can schedule appointments, generate billings, post receivables, keep time records and respond to customer concerns. Will work with minimal supervision, manage time effectively, make independent decisions and meet deadlines. Careful with office equipment.

Willing to adjust work schedule to meet employer's needs.

Honest, dependable, organized, team player.

David Kurtz   Home (317) 546-1890
                                                    Message (317) 986-7600

Position Desired   Electronics Technician

Skills: Over 3 years of directly related skills and educational experiences.
        Vocational school graduate (B+ average). Can operate oscilloscope and
        varied testing equipment, read schematics, design and troubleshoot ana-
        log/digital circuitry, apply basic computer skills. Can logically analyze infor-
        mation, plan and organize daily work, keep accurate and detailed records,
        follow directions. Safety minded and careful with equipment.

Willing to travel, work holidays and weekends, work any shift.

Reliable   Career Minded   Fast Learner   Excited About the Field

---

SARAH WHITAKER   **(812) 654-1764 (H)**
                                                    (812) 647-9214 (M)

Employment Goal: Cabinet Making/General Carpentry/
                     Woodworking

Special Skills: Over 5 years of paid/nonpaid work and on-the-job
                     training using skills and equipment. Can safely
                     operate joiner/planer, assorted power saws, drill
                     press, lathes, etc. Can design, build, laminate, and
                     install custom orders. Will match materials, com-
                     plete trim and finish work. Able to read blueprints,
                     set trusses, and frame. Can meet deadlines, cost
                     out and purchase supplies.

Will work until job is correct and will work weekends.

Quality Minded. Will Work for Every Penny of My Pay.

Juanita C. Navarro   (215) 257-3333
                                                    (215) 632-1190

OBJECTIVE
Seeking a position on a public relations or business communications
staff.

SKILLS
Able to research, write, and edit news releases, news and feature articles,
and advertisements. Capable of designing and preparing brochures and
pamphlets.

EXPERIENCE
Have developed journalism background by working on two high school
publications, doing market research, and interning on a magazine.
Degree: A.B. Journalism, Indiana University, 1991.

STRENGTHS
Am creative, responsible, cooperative, organized, and honest.

Making Your JIST Cards

In pencil, enter information on your own practice JIST card (page 61). Complete the sections one by one, just as they are presented in the chapter. Don't jump ahead. If you have trouble, refer to the sample JIST cards on pages 58–59 for ideas. Also, note that there are a few extra copies of the practice card at the back of your book. If you make some mistakes or see ways to improve on your first attempt, you can use them to start fresh.

JIST Card Sections

Every JIST card has ten parts that you need to consider and develop.

JIST Card Format

1. Name and phone numbers
2. Target heading
3. Job objective
4. Value heading
5. Experience statement
6. Educational statement
7. Job-related skills statement
8. Transferable skills statement
9. Problem-solving statement
10. Self-management skills statement

Try to identify each of these ten parts in the sample cards on the preceding pages. In developing your own JIST card, you should give serious consideration to each section. Follow the directions carefully, and again remember to enter your information in pencil. (You may want to change it later.)

Name and Phone Number(s) The first step in making your own JIST card is to tell the employer who you are. Print your name in the Name space provided on your practice card. Introduce yourself with your proper name. Do not use nicknames.

After stating your name, tell the employer how to contact you. Print your phone number in the Home Phone space on your practice card. If someone is taking messages for you when you are unavailable, enter that person's number in the Message Phone space. (Notice on Sarah Whitaker's sample card on the preceding page that *H* and *M* can be used to signify home and message phone numbers, if you wish.)

Since an employer may only call once, you can't afford to miss a call. If you do not have a phone, list the number of a reliable friend or relative. Be sure to tell the person that you are expecting calls from employers, and give him or her a JIST card or two.

Target Heading Now the employer knows your name and how to contact you. But what do you want? You want a job. Call this to the employer's attention with your Target Heading entry.

PRACTICE JIST CARD

(Name)   (Home Phone)

(Message Phone)

(LEAVE SPACE)

(Target Heading)   (Job Objective)

(LEAVE SPACE)

(Value Heading)   (Experience Statement)

(Education Statement)

(Job-Related Skills Statement)

(Transferable Skills Statement)

(LEAVE SPACE)

(Problem-Solving Statement)

(LEAVE SPACE)

(Self-Management Skills Statement)

Below is a list of target headings used by other successful job seekers through the years. Choose one of these headings, or create your own. Then neatly enter your choice on your practice card.

• Vocational Objective	• Employment Goal
• Employment Objective	• Field of Interest
• Job Objective	• Field of Experience
• Career Objective	• Employment Focus
• Work Objective	• Career Focus
• Vocational Target	• Career Path
• Job Target	• Career Direction
• Target Job	

Job Objective Statement   Print the title of the job you want in the Job Objective section of your practice card. You may choose to include more than one title. If the jobs that interest you are quite different, consider making a separate card for each position.

Value Heading   Your Value Heading entry does just what the name implies—it alerts an employer to your *value* as a worker. It prepares him or her for the powerful information that will follow on your JIST card. Under your value heading, you will write statements about your experience, education, and skills.

Enter your value heading in the space provided on your practice card. Select one of the following examples or make up your own.

• Experiences	• Proven Capabilities
• Proven Experiences	• Proven Worth
• Related Experiences	• Proven Value
• Successful Experiences	• Related Abilities
• Skills	• Areas of Expertise
• Related Skills	• Accomplishments
• Supporting Skills	• Achievements
• Special Skills	• Successes
• Skills/Experience	• Success Patterns
• Knowledge/Skills	• Background
• Capabilities	

Experience Statement   Now tell the employer what you have to offer. On your practice card, this information is entitled Experience Statement. This part of your JIST card tells the employer how long you've been using similar or related skills and where those skills were developed and used (paid work experience, unpaid work experience, related training or education, hobbies, etc.). Take a look at the sample cards on pages 58–59 to see how others have developed their experience statements. If you find one you like, use it. Otherwise develop your own. This is the most important part of your JIST card, so take your time and be careful.

First show your total experience. This should be the length of time you have spent doing things related to your desired job. On the following form, figure your total experience in months and years.

	Years	Months
Related paid employment (includes military experience)	_____	_____
Related unpaid employment (volunteer work, hobbies, and other informal, related work)	_____	_____
Related education and training	_____	_____
Total Related Experience	_____	_____

Note that you may not want to include your total experience figure if it is less than six months.

Look at the experience statement on the sample cards. Then enter your own experience statement in the spaces provided on your practice card. Be positive, but don't exaggerate the truth. You'll have to back up everything you write during interviews.

Education Statement   Employers want to know how your education has prepared you for entering the labor market and doing reliable work. If you are a graduate of a technical or business training program, tell the employer. There's no need to name the school, but you must specify the type of training you received and the type of certification or diploma. Naturally, if you have a good grade point average (B or above), list it. If your average was below B, do not list it.

If you are a vocational/technical/business school graduate with a large number of "hands on" hours, you may want to indicate this on your card. For example, you might state, "Vocational/technical school graduate with over 1,500 hands-on hours of training." If you've taken high school or college courses, or have other degrees or certifications that support your job choice, you might want to list them in this section.

If you are a high school graduate without any further formal education, make sure you mention your diploma. If you have no education that shows your value for the job, skip this section. (You'll make up for this minor loss in other sections.)

Take a look at your DataTrakt booklet, Chapter 1, and the JIST card samples for ideas on how you want to tell employers that your education will help you do a good job. Enter your education statement(s) in the appropriate space on your practice card.

Job-Related Skills   The Job-Related Skills section of your JIST card tells an employer whether or not you have the basic skills and knowledge to handle the job for which you are applying. You cannot complete this section unless you know the most important demands of the job. Go back to Chapter 1 and your DataTrakt booklet to review the demands of your job objective and to identify those that you consider most important.

Select five or six of your job-related skills that would be considered most important in your doing a good job. Enter them into your practice card in the Job-Related Skills section. If you have trouble, take a look at the samples provided on pages 58–59.

Transferable Skills Statement   In the Transferable Skills section you will show employers that you have more than just a working knowledge of the job. You will also show them that you will bring transferable skills to your work. These are important skills that most job seekers forget to mention—but not you. Go back through your list of transferable skills on pages 14–15 to select the five or six skills you feel are most powerful and important. Then write them on your practice card.

Problem-Solving Statement   Employers like to know that you are willing to help them solve their problems. Some of the most common work force problems that employers face are these:

- High turnover

- Refusal to work overtime

- Poor attendance

- Tardiness

- Unwillingness to travel

- Unwillingness to relocate

- Refusal to work weekends or holidays

- Inability or refusal to follow directions

- Inability or unwillingness to do quality work

- Inability to get along with co-workers

If you're part of the solution for employers, not part of the problem, say so! Write two or three positive statements, such as "Willing to relocate" or "Will work any shift," in the Problem-Solving section of your practice card.

Self-Management Skills   Over 60 percent of all workers who are fired are fired because they cannot get along with their co-workers, supervisors, and customers. For this reason, the Self-Management Skills section of your JIST card is extremely important. This statement is also important because it's the last statement you will make about how you will fit into a job and a company.

Go back to your Self-Management Skills exercise on page 17 of Chapter 1. From it select three or four of your self-management skills—those that you feel would be most important to your doing a good job and getting along well with other workers and your boss. Enter these skills on the final line of your practice card.

Appearance and Production

Congratulations! You have just completed your first JIST card. You now have a special tool that sets you apart from most job seekers. Before making copies, consider making improvements. Do you want separate cards for various positions, added information, or a different "look"?

Since appearance counts for a great deal in a job search, you should consider ways to improve the overall appearance of your JIST card. First and foremost, have your cards professionally printed. A JIST card is a multipurpose job-search tool. You will use it in numerous ways and distribute it widely. In effect, it's your personal business card. Its preparation is *not* the place to pinch pennies.

Here are some additional tips for producing the most attractive JIST cards possible:

- ***Color.*** Since most of the paper blizzard associated with job searches is black and white, make your card stand out. Consider the use of colors such as beige, light blue, ivory, light yellow, or light gray. These are all conservative business colors that make an impact. (As with clothing, "hot" colors such as red or orange are never acceptable.) Some people even vary the color of the ink used to print the cards. They substitute navy blue or high-gloss dark brown for the traditional black.

- ***Size.*** Most people developing JIST cards use a 3" x 5" format. This doesn't mean that you can't use 4" x 6" cards.

- ***Design.*** In this chapter you've learned one way—and one way only—to design your card. This was done deliberately, to make sure that you included all of the needed information. There are, however, other possibilities. Some people add design elements like borders or icons to their cards. Others select different typefaces, like

boldface or italics, or mix a few different type sizes. The sample card for Juanita Navarro on page 59 shows how you can redesign your JIST card to make it look entirely different from the practice card. It is an example of what can be done with a little extra time and effort.

- *Accuracy.* Whatever you do to give your card a unique look will be wasted if the information on that card is in any way inaccurate. After you write or keyboard your card copy, make sure there are no spelling errors. Reread it carefully, looking for unclear handwriting or typographical errors. Use a dictionary or spell-check program to look up any words you are unsure of.

- *Quality and cost.* Select high-quality card stock when you have your cards printed. If you use the 3" x 5" format, you can make (or have made) a "master" with five cards fitted onto one sheet. Minimizing the number of sheets used for the entire job will cut waste—and your costs. An average price for 500 quick-print cards made from such a master is about $15–$20 if you do all of the keyboarding and layout work. (Add $5 for keyboarding and $10 for borders and layout if you hire outside help.)

So, with your copy in hand, it's time to pick up a phone book and find a printer. Don't delay. Do your JIST cards now. The sooner you have them, the sooner you can put them to good use.

Using Your Jist Card

How exactly *do* you use your JIST cards? The same way any person employed by a firm uses a business card. Suppose, for example, you visit a company but are not allowed to fill out an application. How do you make an impression? How will the person you spoke with remember you? To keep yourself from becoming just another quickly fading memory, you leave the employer your card. But your card has more on it than just your name and number. It contains a personal sales pitch. As you hand it off to the person you spoke with, you might say something like this: "Thanks so much for your time. Really, I *am* interested in working for this company. I'd appreciate it if you could keep my card on file. I'll check back with you again in a couple of weeks." In this situation your JIST card introduces you. It also gives the employer a permanent record of your visit, even without an application.

Check back with companies where you have left JIST cards. You can do this in person, by mail, or by phone. Each contact will make you more familiar to the employer—and emphasize your interest and motivation. This could be of benefit if you eventually get a chance to interview. Your initiative and determination will be established qualities. One word of caution, however—use good judgment about the frequency of your contacts. Do not make a pest of yourself. Appearing overly eager may irritate employers.

In situations where you are given an application, fill it out. *Never* use the JIST card in place of an application. Rather, attach your card to the upper *right-hand* corner of your application with a paper clip or staple. This will set your application apart from others. (To ensure that you are prepared for this turn of events, always carry some paper clips or a small stapler with your JIST cards.)

Distribute your JIST cards among all the people you know who could help you find a job. Give a card to each of your references. These people will be able to use the information on the card to give you good recommendations. Also, give one to each of your friends and relatives. They can use them as a reminder to keep their eyes and ears open for job leads to pass on to you. And be sure to enclose a card with each thank-you note that you send to interviewers. Some job seekers even post cards on grocery store and other bulletin boards.

For your part, remember that the skills and good-qualities statements on your JIST card are part of a new vocabulary you are learning. This vocabulary is especially useful when you are talking to employers. The phrases on your JIST card will become the basis for telephone contacts and interview responses. Not only will you be able to answer questions like "Why should I hire you?" but you'll be able to do it quickly and concisely.

So, be creative with your JIST cards. Throughout your job search, wherever you go, let them draw employers' attention to you. Be generous with your JIST cards, and they will increase your chances of being chosen for interviews.

CHAPTER FIVE

Telephone Contacts

Dialing for Dollars

Only about 25 percent of all available jobs are "visible." These are the jobs that are advertised in newspapers and listed with employment agencies. The average job seeker goes no further. You, however, already know about paper tools (like JIST cards) that set you apart from the competition.

You can also learn how to uncover the job openings that are not made public. These "hidden" jobs are the real gold mine of job seeking, making up 75 percent of all available positions. In this chapter, you will learn an effective way to hunt for this gold mine.

Since so few job openings are made public, you cannot wait to hear about them. Check with the companies you are interested in, whether they have listed openings or not.

One way to contact companies is to visit as many as possible each day. Do you think this would be the most efficient use of your time and effort? No, it would not. You would spend too much time traveling and waiting to see people. You would also find it hard to get past all of those receptionists who try to turn away job seekers. Your JIST card would help in these situations, but you need to talk to the people who do the hiring. Otherwise, your visits will not be ideal contacts.

A more efficient way to approach employers is to use the telephone. Using the telephone in your job search provides the following advantages:

- You can contact many employers in just a few hours each day.

- You can gather information faster and easier.

- You are more likely to contact the person doing the hiring.

- You will know better what to expect when you go for an interview.

- You will save money.

In this chapter you will learn to use an important verbal tool—the telephone contact. For it you will create a phone presentation that will help you get the interviews you want. Your telephone contacts will also produce information that will help you in your job search.

Your telephone presentation will be a brief statement. It will describe who you are, the position you want, and what you have to offer. At the end of your presentation, you will ask for an interview. In this way, you will meet the three major expectations of employers:

- Your *appearance* will be good because you will sound like the kind of person who can do the job.

- You can tell the employer that you are *dependable.* You can also mention other qualities that you have to offer.

- You will be informing the employer about your *skills.*

Your JIST card will help you create your telephone presentation. By now you should have your printed cards. Keep a JIST card handy as you learn the mechanics of telephone contacts.

A good way to start learning how to create and use your own phone presentation is to listen to how one might sound. The example that follows is based on a JIST card from the previous chapter. Notice that the content is similar to John Chen's JIST card (page 58), but it has been changed to sound as though John were speaking. When you read the presentation, imagine that John is calling someone whose name was given to him by a friend. John does not know this person, and there may or may not be a job available.

Here is what John says: "Hello, my name is John Chen. I'm interested in a position as an accountant or bookkeeper. I'm a graduate of a bookkeeping program and have nearly two years of experience in the accounting field. My skills include processing and posting inventory, sales, payables, and payroll. I'm also able to maintain a general ledger, compile special reports, prepare taxes, and use all standard accounting equipment, including computerized systems. I'm organized, reliable, and good at solving problems. When may I come in for an interview?"

How did that sound? If you were the person being called, would you be impressed? If you hired people with the kinds of skills John has, would you agree to see him?

Most people *are* impressed by a phone presentation such as the one above. Some people think that it sounds pushy, but most say John gives the impression that he is organized and qualified for the job. They would be willing to interview him if they had an opening for someone with his skills.

Basic Parts of a Telephone Presentation

A complete telephone presentation has four basic parts:

1. Name—who you are
2. Position—what you want
3. Hook—what you have to offer
4. Goal—an interview

Let's take a closer look at how each part is constructed.

Name

When you talk to someone for the first time, you usually greet the person and introduce yourself. This is common courtesy. When you are making telephone contacts, however, introducing yourself is more than courteous. It's essential. After all, you want potential employers to know and recognize you. So, begin each contact with a greeting and your name.

The common greeting below is recommended for your first telephone contacts. Write your first and last names in the space.

"Hello, my name is _____."

Always remember to give both your first and last names. Do not start the contact on a first-name basis. You are not making a casual call. Everything you say should prove to the employer that you "mean business."

Position

After you introduce yourself, tell the employer what you want. Do not force him or her to guess the reason for your call. You want a job. Be specific but tactful in stating your desire.

The statement below is recommended for your first telephone contacts. Write the job title of the position you want in the blank. Then read the statement aloud to see if it suits you.

"I'm interested in a position as a(n) _____."

Notice that the word *position* is used rather than *job*. This is a tactful way of saying what you want. The employer's response to the word *job* would likely be defensive. Never make statements such as the following:

- "I'm calling about a job."

- "I wonder if you could tell me if you have any jobs?"

- "Do you have a job for me?"

Little things like this make a difference. If you doubt it, make five calls using the recommended statement and five using the word *job*. Compare the results.

Hook

You've now arrived at the most important part of your phone presentation. The hook is a brief statement of your experience and skills. It grabs the attention of the employer and makes him or her want to listen to you. Your hook will set you apart from most applicants, who simply ask for any job and mention no qualifications.

Your hook should show action. Tell the employer what you have done. Then emphasize what you can do and can offer. The following statements are examples of effective hooks.

Machinist: "I have two years' experience as a machinist's helper. I can operate various drill presses, punch presses, lathes, and saws. I'm very accurate and a hard worker."

Beginner: "I'm dependable, healthy, and eager to learn—and I believe in doing good day's work for my wages."

To write your own hook, use the skills and experience statements from your JIST card. These statements should already be brief and complete. You need only put them into a conversational form.

For example, this hook is based on the JIST card that appears below: "I have two years of experience working on American and foreign-made cars. I can use all hand and power tools commonly used in auto repair. I'm experienced in tune-ups, good with customers, and exact when handling cash. You'll find me reliable, prompt, and willing to learn."

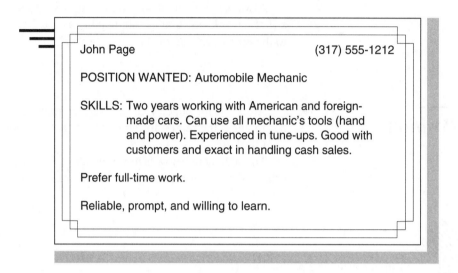

John Page   (317) 555-1212

POSITION WANTED: Automobile Mechanic

SKILLS: Two years working with American and foreign-
         made cars. Can use all mechanic's tools (hand
         and power). Experienced in tune-ups. Good with
         customers and exact in handling cash sales.

Prefer full-time work.

Reliable, prompt, and willing to learn.

Read the skills and experience portions of your JIST card aloud. You may want to change some of the wording as you read. When you are comfortable with the sound of your hook, write it below.

My Hook

_____

_____

_____

_____

_____

_____

_____

Goal

Your primary goal for each phone contact is to get an interview. How you state your goal will depend on whether you know the person you are calling, have been referred by someone, or have simply found his or her name in the phone book. The methods you use to handle each situation will be reviewed in detail later in this chapter.

Remember what John Chen said in the sample phone contact used earlier: "When can I come in for an interview?" This question is short, direct, and clear. There is no doubt about what John wants—an interview. You will use similar statements in your phone contacts.

Getting an interview will always be the main goal of your phone contacts, but there are actually three additional goals. They are (in order of importance) referrals, information, and help.

Main Goal: An Interview Always ask three times for an interview, if necessary. If no jobs are available now, ask to interview for future openings. If the person is too busy to see you, offer to see him or her the following week or as soon as it is convenient. If the person is unwilling to set up an appointment now, ask if it would be okay to check back. Then set a date and time, and call back as promised.

Goal #2: A Referral If you can't get an interview, try to get a referral. Ask if the person knows anyone else, either in the same organization or in any other, who might use someone with your skills.

Goal #3: Information If you can't get an interview or a referral, try to get useful information about the person's organization or similar organizations. You might also ask the best ways to get started in the field.

Goal #4: Advice and Future Help Finally, if all else fails, try to get some advice about your job-search efforts. Request a critique of your phone presentation. Ask, "Do I sound like a person who would fit into this field if you were hiring?" You might also try to get a promise of future assistance by asking to call back at a later date.

Your Telephone Presentation

Based on what you have learned so far, write out your own phone presentation in the space below.

MY PHONE PRESENTATION

Name: "Hello, my name is _____."

Position: "I'm interested in a position as a(n) _____."

Hook: _____

_____

_____

_____

_____

_____

_____

_____

_____

Goal: _____

_____

You may have to write out your own phone presentation several times before it sounds right. Read it aloud after you have written it down. Does it sound natural? Have you written it the way you would speak it? Keep making changes until it sounds just right.

If you have trouble perfecting your presentation, ask your instructor or a friend for help. Rehearse your presentation with friends and family. The more you say it aloud, the more natural it will sound and feel to you.

You will need to use good judgment about when you should offer to call back rather than ask for an interview. Role-playing phone contacts will help you develop a good sense of the best strategy for each case.

Be sure you learn to ask for an interview at least three times before accepting "no" as an answer. You will be amazed how often "no" turns to "yes" when you ask that third time.

Send thank-you notes to anyone who is at all helpful. Insert a JIST card and a resume, and plan to recontact anyone who seems to be a possible employer.

30 Seconds— Count!

Your telephone presentation should be designed to quickly attract an employer's attention to you and your special qualifications. As you practice it, time yourself. You should be able to deliver your full presentation in 30 seconds. Don't rush, however. Just be natural.

If you find that you are being interrupted before you finish, you need more practice. Pauses in your presentation give employers a chance to say, "Sorry, no openings." You don't want an employer to speak until you've stated your name, position, hook, and goal.

At first it may be obvious that you are reading your telephone presentation. Don't be too concerned. It will become more natural the more you use it.

Vim and Vigor

How interested are you in getting a job? Do you really want to work? Your answers may show how enthusiastic you are. Enthusiasm is important in a job search. It will be reflected in your voice as you make your phone contacts.

Knowing and practicing your phone presentation will increase your confidence. However, you must show your spirit with your voice. If you sound uninterested, you will probably get an uninterested response. If you sound sad, you may arouse an employer's sympathy. Sadness, however, does not qualify you for a job. With vim and vigor in your voice, you will sound like the person interested in doing the best job.

Practice your presentation in front of a friend. Ask how you sound. If possible, record your presentation on a tape recorder. Listen to the recording and decide whether or not you sound convincing. (If you don't have a tape recorder, borrow one from a friend or the public library.)

Some Things to Remember

When making a telephone contact, be brief and to the point. Sound businesslike, but do not be abrupt. And do not let an employer interview you on the phone. (Very few people are hired over the phone.)

Always your objective is to talk to the most knowledgeable people in the field—bosses and employers. Always your objective is to get an interview. Failing that, you want to learn as much as you can about your field—and you should say so.

Do not address the person you are calling by his or her first name. Doing so may make the person uncomfortable. It may also give the impression that you are too aggressive or too casual.

If you are calling from home, keep background noises to a minimum. Remember, it's difficult to sound focused and professional with music blaring in the background or children crying for attention. Don't let background noise screen you out of an interview before you've even finished your presentation.

When you do get an appointment for an interview, always repeat the date, time, and address to confirm them. Also, repeat the interviewer's name—and write down everything!

Advanced Phone Techniques

Having now mastered your basic phone presentation, you can benefit from learning some of the finer points of contacting employers by phone. The remaining parts of this chapter provide helpful tips for making successful phone contacts.

Telephoning Friends and Relatives

Among the best sources of job leads are the people you know. You will begin your phone contacts with these people more informally than you will begin contacts with people you don't know. If the person you are calling knows you well, you might say, "Hi, this is Jane Marrin (use your own name here, of course)." You will probably make small talk for a while, and then, as soon as possible, get to the point. If the person you are calling does not hire people with your skills, present your hook as you wrote it and ask the person if he or she knows of anyone who might be able to help you. Since your contacts very often will not know of anyone, ask another question, such as, "Do you know anyone else who might know someone who needs a worker with my skills?" Often this question will produce a name even if the first question didn't.

Getting to the Person Who Can Hire You

In Chapter 7 you will learn more about asking your friends and relatives to help you obtain interviews. You will also learn more about going directly to employers to ask for interviews. Much of what follows in this chapter assumes that you are contacting employers whom you do not know. It is best to be referred to these employers by someone who knows them, but this is not always possible. The techniques for finding which employers to contact will be reviewed in Chapter 7. For now, assume that you have taken the names from the Yellow Pages of the phone book.

Your primary goal is to get an interview. Ideally you want to speak to the person who can both interview and hire you. Ask to speak to that person before you begin your phone presentation.

Perhaps you know the name of the supervisor for the job you want. You may have learned it from family or friends. If you know that person's name, use it. Say, "Hello, I would like to speak with (person's name)."

If you do not know the name you need, ask to speak to the right person by title. Most companies are organized into departments or units. A manager, supervisor, or director is in charge of a particular department. Ask to speak with that person. You can say, "Hello, I would like to speak with the manager (supervisor, director) of the _____ department, please. Could you tell me that person's name?" Once you reach the right person, give your presentation.

If possible, avoid the personnel department. Most applicants either ask to speak to someone in personnel or are automatically transferred there because they say, "I'm looking for a job." The personnel department has many more applicants than jobs. Therefore, it rejects more applicants than it accepts. You do not want to be screened out. If your call is routed to personnel, however, follow through with your presentation.

Each phone contact will test your presentation. If you are constantly being interrupted, practice more. If you are getting interviews, you will probably be offered a job soon.

Getting Past the Secretary

When you make a phone contact, you will usually speak to a secretary or receptionist first. The secretary cannot hire you, so ask for the person who can. Most secretaries will then ask what business you have with that person. How will you state your business?

Suppose you have been referred to this employer by someone who knows him or her. Simply say, "I was referred to Mr. Jones by a friend of his, Ann Rhodes, who suggested that Mr. Jones could help me." This technique will usually get you through to the person you want to talk to.

If you have not been referred to an employer by someone he or she knows, consider the following techniques:

- *Tell the secretary that you are seeking a position with the company.* This is true. However, your call may be channeled to the personnel department rather than to the person you want.

- *Say that your business is personal.* This also is true and will likely get you to your connection. Although this technique works, some employers may see it as a trick and not like it. If they take your call and then find out that they do not have a personal relationship with you, they may form a lasting negative impression of you.

- *Be creative.* Call to discuss an issue important to the employer. Someone applying for a job as secretary might make the following creative statement: "I'm calling about ways to increase administrative support for line staff."

Whatever reason you give for wishing to speak to the right person, sound businesslike. You will be less apt to get the "runaround."

Shotgunning and Throwaway Calls

If you still have trouble contacting the right person, try "shotgunning." With this technique, you use your presentation on each person with whom you talk. In this way you avoid asking for specific people. You also avoid questions about why you are calling.

Shotgunning depends on the element of surprise. With each person who answers the phone, as fast as 1-2-3-4, you fire off your name, position, hook, and goal. Bang! You confront each person with the unexpected—a job seeker with a dynamite presentation. These people will have to react.

If you choose this method, chances are you will sometimes be routed to personnel. However, some people will connect you to the person with whom you wish to speak. Why? Simply because you have not called to ask if somebody, somewhere, could give you just any kind of job. Rather, you have presented yourself as a unique person with something to offer.

Another good reason for using shotgunning is that small organizations usually do not have a personnel office. It is often very easy to get to the hiring authority.

When you use shotgunning, do the following:

- *Use your basic phone presentation on everyone.*

- *Write down the name of each person with whom you speak.* You will then be prepared if you must retrace your steps. If names are not volunteered, ask.

- *If you are routed to the personnel department, give your presentation.* It's a gamble, but you have nothing to lose. Perhaps there is an opening. If not, you will have gained helpful practice.

After you have memorized your presentation, the best practice is to make throwaway calls. Throwaway calls are those in which the outcome is not important. Call the organization lowest on your list of possible employers. If you don't get an interview, you won't be disappointed. If you do get one, you'll have an opportunity to practice your interview skills. And you might just get a job offer!

Dealing with "Sorry, No Openings"

During your presentation someone may say, "Sorry, no openings." A secretary may say it or an employer—it doesn't matter. What does matter is how you react. Average job seekers quit at this point. If someone tells you there are no openings after you have given your phone presentation, show that person that you merit a second look. Consider the following responses.

Response #1: "I *am* very interested in working for your company. When may I call back concerning the position I want?" This shows your motivation and persistence. It compliments the employer's company. It gives you another chance. Get a specific date and write it down. Then call back as scheduled.

Response #2: "I'm sure my skills will apply to other positions. What positions are available? When may I come in to discuss them with you?" This demonstrates your flexibility, initiative, and knowledge of what you can do.

Response #3: "I understand that there are no openings now, but I would still like to interview with you for future positions that might open up." Remember that your primary goal in making the phone contact is to get an interview. Do not take the first no as an acceptable answer. Very often if you ask again after a first or even second no, you will get an interview.

Response #4: If you do not get an interview after asking several times, you can always ask something like this: "Do you know of any companies similar to yours that would be interested in a person with my skills?" This shows your initiative and motivation. It may also get you valuable job leads. When someone tells you about other companies, ask for names of persons to contact.

These responses may be used separately or in combination. Practice saying them aloud. One of these questions could turn a dead-end call into a productive one.

Following Up

Following up on your phone contacts can make the difference in whether or not you get a job. Following up is necessary in the two situations described below.

When You Get an Interview If you get an interview, make sure you know the name of the person who will be interviewing you. You must also know the correct date, time, and address. Unless the interview is within the next several days, send a thank-you note, a JIST Card, and a resume to help the interviewer prepare for the interview. Send these paper tools the same day that you get the interview.

When You Don't Get an Interview Suppose you don't get an interview because the key person is busy when you call, but you do arrange for a follow-up call. Send a thank-you note. Thank that person for his or her interest, and enclose a JIST card and resume. Also, send a thank-you note if someone simply refers you to someone else. Send one even if someone refuses to see you (at least the person took your call). It is just good manners to thank people who help you in any way. It is also true that people are far more likely to remember you when jobs do open up if you have taken the time to thank them. If you sent your JIST card along with a thank-you note, they will have your phone number when they need it.

Getting an In-Person Interview

If you construct your phone presentation with care and practice it well, you will probably be invited to interview. This should be an in-person interview, however. Remember, do not allow yourself to be interviewed on the phone.

Nonetheless, you should be prepared to answer (and ask) certain questions during your phone contacts. Here are three areas in which you should have responses planned. Write your answers in the spaces provided.

ANSWERS TO PREDICTABLE PHONE REQUESTS

"Briefly expand on the skills you have already presented."

_____

_____

_____

_____

"Briefly expand on why you would be a good employee."

_____

_____

_____

"What questions do you have about the company and the job you are seeking?"
(*Caution:* Do *not* ask about pay at this time).

_____

_____

_____

To avoid being caught in a telephone interview, just answer basic questions. Then say, "Perhaps we could discuss my qualifications further—when I come in for an interview." If all goes smoothly, the employer will react to you rather than you to him. Thus, an interview will be scheduled. Be sure to write down the interviewer's name, and the date, time, and address of the interview.

Now, practice your basic telephone presentation. Also, practice what you will say when the employer wants to interview you or questions you on the phone.

Overcoming Fears

Making phone contacts is hard for most people. Why? Because they are afraid they will make someone angry or embarrass themselves.

The truth is, however, that very few employers will be rude to you. Smart employers are always interested in hearing from people with the skills they need to run their businesses. And they are often willing to see you even when they have no openings! They will do this to consider you for future positions, help you out with a referral, or give you other support.

Experience with phone contacts has shown that it takes 10–15 calls to get one interview—and that's in a good economy. This means that even in the best of circumstances you will hear the word *no* more than the word *yes*. While this may sound discouraging, consider that you can easily make 10 phone calls an hour. At that rate, you could get two interviews in just a few hours. If you did this every day, you would have 10 interviews a week, or 40 a month. Those kinds of numbers will get you a job very quickly.

6

CHAPTER SIX

The Interview

For Rave Reviews

Doing well in a job interview is essential to getting most jobs. Very few people are hired without first being interviewed. The time you spend interviewing is the most important time in your job search.

In a typical situation, the interviewer will be considering a number of people for one job. He or she will need to eliminate everyone from consideration except the one person who is eventually hired. This means that the interviewer will try to find weaknesses in each applicant.

If this sounds unfriendly, it is! Keep in mind that an interview is really a business transaction. You offer something of value (your service) in exchange for money (the employer's job opening). There is more to it than this, of course, but value for pay is the basis of the hiring decision.

Interviews last from 15 minutes to well over an hour. (Most last 30–45 minutes.) If you aren't screened out in the first interview, you will often be asked back for a second or even a third interview before you are offered a job.

Job interviews usually end in one of three ways:

• The employer offers the applicant a job.

• The employer rejects the applicant, or the applicant rejects the job.

• No decision is made until a future date.

The last is the most common of the three results.

In the interview competition, you will have a number of advantages over most job seekers. You know what employers look for in the people they hire, and you know enough about yourself to tell employers what you have to offer.

Meeting Employer Expectations

You were introduced to the three major expectations of employers at the beginning of this book. You have since touched on them many times. An interview, however, is a special situation. Nowhere else in the job-search process do those expectations come together with such force and concentration. In a limited period of time, you must make yourself stand out from all the competition. How? By impressing the employer with your appearance, dependability, and skills.

Appearance

Do you remember the four aspects of good appearance? They are the way you look, behave, write, and speak. Chapter 1 discussed the way you look in some detail and provided rules for dress, grooming, and personal hygiene. (You may want to go back and review those rules now.) Chapter 2 dealt with the way you present yourself on paper. It also introduced a tool—the DataTrakt—to help you produce applications that are neat, complete, and accurate every time. In this chapter, we'll concentrate on the remaining two aspects of appearance—the way you behave and the way you speak.

The Way You Behave At an interview you will be observed from the moment you enter the door. Walk in with confidence and energy. Greet the secretary or receptionist with a smile. Tell this person your name and the reason you are there. Say, for example, "Good morning, my name is Charles Attwood. I'm here to interview for the assembler position." Or say, "Hello. I'm Trisha Conner. I have a 3 p.m. appointment with Mrs. Ford."

You should arrive 10–15 minutes early. Use this time wisely. Take notice of the surroundings. Look for reading material. Do not pace the floor. Be calm and look smart. The employer may not be watching you, but the secretary probably will be. He or she might describe your waiting-room manner to the employer.

When you are called in for your interview, greet the employer with a firm handshake and a smile. Be ready with an opening statement. An example would be "Good day, Mr. Jones. My name is Charles Attwood." Never use the employer's first name—you are not old friends yet. Do not sit down until the employer offers you a seat. If the employer does not offer one, ask if you may sit down. Sit up straight or lean slightly forward in your chair to show your interest. Keep your feet on the floor and your hands in your lap. Use gestures and body movements to express yourself, but do not be extreme. Look the interviewer in the eye to show that you are honest and confident. However, do not stare. If you find it hard to keep eye contact, look at the interviewer's nose or eyebrows.

Always be alert. This shows that you are eager to learn and succeed. Afterwards, be sure to thank the employer for the time and consideration given you.

The Way You Speak Most employers want to hire workers with good verbal communication skills—for all jobs. These employers believe that their businesses will run more smoothly and more profitably if their workers can communicate effectively. They want workers who do the following when they speak:

- Pronounce words clearly and confidently so that everyone can understand

- Speak in complete, logical sentences so that there is no doubt about the meaning of what's being said

- Show enthusiasm and spirit when they talk

- Use correct grammar

- Speak honestly and openly, rather than "beating around the bush" or avoiding tough questions

Dependability

Dependability is the second employer expectation. You may be asking, "How can I show *that* in an interview?" To start, just by showing up and being on time.

A second way is to *tell* your interviewer that you are dependable and punctual and to support your statements. Say, "I'm a well-organized person. I've always been on time in coming to work, keeping my appointments, and turning in my reports. Punctuality is very important to me, and I'm proud of my record." Or you can say, "My last employer used to laugh and say he didn't need a watch to tell what time it was because I always walked through the door at 7:45."

In Chapter 1 you listed examples and wrote some statements to illustrate your good attendance, punctuality, and reliability. Now would be a good time to refresh your memory by reviewing those statements. And if you can think of any ways to improve them— by all means, do so.

Skills

Interviewers want to know if your skills qualify you for a certain job. They are looking for someone with the right skills and qualifications, and the ability to learn the necessary new skills. Interviewers ask questions to find out about your skills. However, some things will not be covered unless you mention them. You have a lot to offer employers. It is up to you to say so during an interview. Now is a good time to review previous chapters and your job-seeking tools. You should find several well-organized lists of your most relevant skills.

It is important that you make several different skills statements during an interview. You must do this to let your interviewer know you are the right person for the job. Tell how you used your skills in former positions. And above all, make your skills statements positive. Remember, one small bit of negative data carries more weight than a huge piece of positive information.

Talk about your skills *early* in an interview. Do this in as many different ways as possible. Why? Because employers tend to make decisions within the first 4–9 minutes. If you compile a group of skills statements, you will have a powerful message for those first, critical minutes of an interview.

As an exercise, assemble your strongest skills statements from this book and from your job-search tools. Try to improve each statement as you write it here. Always be complete, accurate, and positive. Remember that each statement must relate to the job for which you are applying. If a statement does not apply, list another skill instead.

MY STRONGEST SKILLS STATEMENTS

I'm good at.

Job-related skills statement: _____

_____

_____

Transferable skills statement: _____

_____

_____

supervision

Self-management skills statement: _____

_____

_____

Mastering Key Interview Techniques

By now you should know which of your qualifications best relate to the job you want. You should also be able to present your qualifications as answers to an interviewer's questions.

The best way to sort and assemble your data is to relate it to specific questions an interviewer will probably ask. The true test of your skills statements will be how well you meet employer expectations in the face of difficult questions.

Using Proof-by-Example

Proof-by-example is an important interview strategy. It will provide you with an easy way to give powerful responses to almost any interview question. Without knowing it you've actually been using the proof-by-example technique since Chapter 1. Remember, there you learned about the importance of using specific examples to support all of your skills and experience statements.

Suppose you're asked the following question in an interview: "Why don't you tell me about yourself?" Most job seekers would not handle this question well. But here's how a person using the proof-by-example approach might answer: "Well, you probably want to know what sort of worker I am. I'm the kind of person who likes to do things well and on time. For example, in a previous job I was given the responsibility of finishing an important project after another person left the company. I had to stay up nights revising the plans for a job our company was bidding on. All of this was new to me, but I finished the project on time and we were awarded a contract worth over a million dollars. I feel I can use the same skills and hard work to do well on this job, too."

Sounds good, doesn't it? Let's break down this person's response so that we can look at it more closely. Assign points to the proof-by-example steps as shown below. Using this system, a score of ten would be the highest possible score for any one response. Such a score would mean that the speaker had done an excellent job in developing a solid interview answer.

Proof-by-Example Strategy

Steps	Points
1. *Provide a good example of a key skill.* By now you know the skills needed on the job for which you are interviewing. You should also have a variety of examples of how and where you have used those skills in the past. Select one skill and at least three examples that illustrate your success in applying it.	2
2. *Give details.* For each example provide enough details to make an interesting but short story. Tell as much as is necessary about who, what, where, when, and why for the story to make sense.	2
3. *Use numbers or other measurable data.* People will pay more attention if you use some numbers to support your story. Talk about dollars saved, number of people served, percentage of sales increased, budget per year, or increased orders. Use any numbers or pieces of data that you can think of!	2
4. *Mention results.* Did your work accomplish the intended purpose? Tell how you know.	2
5. *Link and think.* Look for a way to connect what you did in your example with doing a good job in the position for which you are interviewing. The more specific you can be, the better.	2
Total	10

You can improve your interviewing skills simply by scoring your responses in terms of the steps described on page 82. If you included a step, give yourself a point. If you did a very good job of meeting the step's requirements, give yourself another point. How many points would you have given the response of the job seeker quoted on page 82, the one who "likes to do things well and on time"?

Handling Problem Questions

A problem question is a question that the average job seeker would find difficult to answer in a positive way. You should expect several problem questions in each interview. However, no question will pose a real problem if you are prepared to answer it. In fact, most interview questions should help you tell how you meet an employer's expectations.

Understanding which employer expectation is actually behind a problem question will help you make the best possible answer. For example, if the interviewer asks why you left your last job, he or she is probably trying to find out whether or not you are dependable. Knowing this will help you answer the question in a way that says you will meet that employer expectation. You might say, "I left my last job because I decided that my long-term career goal was to be a _____. I took several classes to prepare myself for the change in jobs and saved for many months to prepare for a full-time job search. I know I did the right thing and am looking forward to a position in this field."

Whatever your situation, you must find ways to present yourself in the most positive way. When the facts are not positive, it is best to be honest. Then quickly present what you learned from the situation to help you do well in this job.

To prepare for interviews, you should become familiar with typical interview questions. The following pages contain lists of them. As you read through these lists, note any question that might be difficult for you to answer. Think about, write down, and then practice presenting positive answers.

This first list includes some of the most common interview questions that job seekers often have trouble answering:

- "Won't you tell me about yourself?"

- "Why have you held so many jobs?"

- "What is your major weakness?"

- "How much do you expect to be paid?"

- "Why do you want to work for this company?"

- "Why did you leave your last job?"

- "Why do you have this gap in your job history?"

- "What are your future plans?"

- "What do you like to do in your leisure time?"

Because these questions are asked so often, we'll consider each of them separately.

"Won't You Tell Me About Yourself?"   This may be one of an interviewer's first questions. The interviewer is not asking for your life history. Rather, he or she is trying to find out about your job skills. The question also allows the interviewer to see how well you express yourself. It has several variations:

- "Why should I hire you?"

- "What is your experience?"

- "Tell me about other jobs you have had."

Be prepared to give the entire series of statements about your best qualifications for the job. Be specific and include examples to support your claims. With every response, try to show that you meet one or more of the three major employer expectations. Before responding to the question in the exercise space below, you may want to review some of your responses to exercises in Chapter 1.

Now take the time to make your own response as complete, accurate, and positive as possible. Note that the question lets you talk about your dedication to attendance, punctuality, and dependability, as well as your skills. Use the five-step, proof-by-example approach. Ready?

Employer: "Won't you tell me about yourself?"

(loud)

Your response: _____

_____

_____

_____

_____

_____

"Why Have You Held So Many Jobs?" Today's workers will have, on average, eight job changes in their working lives. The average job in the United States lasts only a little over four years. Given these figures, *have* you had an unusual number of jobs? If not, you may never be asked the question.

If an interviewer does ask why you have had so many jobs, explain that you have kept your jobs as long as the average, or longer. Assure the interviewer that you intend to stay with this new job for quite some time. Tell him or her that this is the job you want and that you can do it well. Emphasize your dependability.

Job seekers who have had many jobs in a short time tend to follow one of two patterns. In one pattern the job seekers take different kinds of jobs. In the other pattern they do the same kind of job but change employers often. At first glance, neither type appears dependable. Both need to give good reasons for leaving their previous jobs— and both potentially have them.

If you have had many different kinds of jobs, you may have been deciding on a career. A positive reason for your job history could be that you were exploring different kinds of work. In your various jobs you have gained skills, abilities, experience, and training that relate to the job you seek.

Downsized

Suppose your work record shows that you have always had the same kind of job but at different companies. A positive reason for this pattern could be that you wanted to move up more quickly than staying at one place would allow. Of course, to support this answer you would have to show that you've held a series of increasingly responsible positions. If not, the suspicion might be that you quit or were fired.

Your DataTrakt and application should show employers that there were no negative reasons for your leaving past jobs. However, if you think a former employer will speak negatively of you, cover yourself in the interview. People are usually fired because personal, nonwork problems interfere with their work. If you must mention a personal problem, be general and brief. Explain that the problem has been resolved. Note in the following examples that words like *fired* or *quit* are never used.

- "I left my job because I was going through a divorce. I went back to work as soon as that problem was completely resolved."

- "I was involved in an auto accident and had to stay home for several months. After recovering completely, I resumed work."

- "A few years back I had a drinking problem and missed some work. However, I joined A.A. and haven't touched a drop in three years now. In my present position, I've received two annual bonus checks for perfect attendance."

After describing your problem and how you resolved it, get right back to outlining your qualifications.

Respond to the following question if it applies to you. If it does not, go to the next section.

Employer: "Why have you held so many jobs?

Your response: _____

_____

_____

"What Is Your Major Weakness?"   This question is designed to give the interviewer negative information about you. It also tests your ability to handle tough questions. Stick to job-related information. *Never* be negative. Rather, turn any negatives into positives. Turn your weaknesses into strengths. Here are some examples.

- *Weakness:*   "I'm too slow."

   Positive statement: "I'm sometimes too careful about my work. I'll work late to get my job done just right."

- *Weakness:*   "I don't like people telling me what to do."

   Positive statement: "I tend to ask a lot of questions about what I'm told to do. That way I can be sure I'll do it right."

Do not tell the interviewer that you have no weaknesses. If you cannot think of one, say something positive about yourself. For example, say, "Maybe it would be my endless curiosity. I really like to know how things work."

Now try your hand at turning negatives into positives.

Employer: "What is your major weakness?"

Your response: _____

_____

_____

"How Much Do You Expect to Be Paid?" A poor response to the salary question can turn out to be a very expensive lesson. Unless you are being offered a job, don't talk about salary at all. Whatever you say about money in an early interview will probably screen you out of the job.

Let's say that the employer is willing to pay $10 per hour, but you say you will accept $6. What do you think you will be paid if you get the job? You should also realize that answering $6 in this situation may actually prevent you from getting the job. The employer may keep looking for a person who thinks he or she is worth more than you think you are worth. It can work just this way!

Of course, your answer can work against you if you say that you are looking for a higher salary than the interviewer has in mind. He or she might just keep looking for a person who would be happy with what the job pays.

You might try a neutral statement that does not commit you either way. For example, say, "I would expect to be paid what other persons in this job are paid." Sometimes it is best to answer this question with another question. The simplest replies would be "How much does the job pay?" or "How much is a new employee in this position usually paid?" If you have experience in the same kind of job, you might say, "How much do you usually pay someone with my experience?" Answering the question with a question may get you a salary higher than what you would have received otherwise.

Another good approach is to mention a salary range that probably includes the salary the employer is considering but also goes higher. For example, if you think the employer will probably pay an annual salary of about $15,000, you might say that you are looking for a salary in the midteens to lower twenties. This answer covers a huge range ($13,000–$24,000) and should let you move on to more important topics.

Which type of response do you think is best for you? Try it out here.

Employer: "How much do you expect to be paid?"

Your response: _____

_____

_____

"Why Do You Want to Work for This Company?" This question presents a problem only if you do not expect it to be asked. Also, if you are not prepared, you will miss your chance to compliment the company and, thus, the interviewer. The interviewer does not necessarily ask the question to get a compliment. However, your answer should always include one. The interviewer expects you to show your interest. You can do this with an answer that indicates you have researched the company.

Research each company before you go to an interview. You can do this in many different ways. Most research takes very little time. It can make the difference in whether or not you are hired. (See Chapter 7.)

Visit the company. If you know people who work there, talk to them. Ask employees with jobs similar to the one you want what they like about the company. This gives you a ready answer to the interviewer's question. You can say, "I've talked with some of your employees, and they feel this is a good company to work for because . . ."

Read company newsletters and financial reports. You can then say something like this in an interview: "I've been reading that Newstar is really growing fast. That's one of the reasons I want to work for the company—because it has a great future and can offer me a chance to grow with it." Write your own version of this response at the top of the following page.

Employer: "Why do you want to work for this company?"

Your response: _____

_____

_____

_____

"Why Did You Leave Your Last Job?"   The employer asks this question to find out if you had any problems on your last job. If you did, you may have the same problems on a new job. Following are some tips on how to answer this question.

- *Never say anything negative about yourself or your previous employer.* If you did have problems, think of a way to explain them without being negative.

- *Be very careful not to use the word* **fired** *when explaining why you left a previous job.* Perhaps you were "laid off" or your position was "cut." Use these words to explain what happened.

- *If you were fired and are not on good terms with your previous employer, maybe you should explain.* First examine why you were fired. Try to learn something from the situation. Were you partly to blame? If you have learned something from the situation, explain this honestly. Avoid criticizing your employer. The odds are good that the interviewer has been fired at some time, too. He or she may understand your situation better than you expect.

Many people are fired because nonwork matters interfere with their on-the-job performance. Did a divorce or something happening in your personal life cause you to be fired? Have you resolved the problem? If so, let your interviewer know this. Tell him or her that the former problem will not affect your work.

Prepare a positive explanation, if possible. Practice answering this question below.

Employer: "Why did you leave your last job?" _____

Your response: _____

_____

_____

_____

"Why Do You Have This Gap in Your Job History?"   Questions about job gaps are very important questions. How you answer these questions is even more important. If you have not been out of work for more than three months, don't worry. U.S. Labor Department statistics show that the average period of unemployment between jobs is 3–4 months (*Employment and Earnings Bulletin,* Vol. 25, No. 1). You might point this out to the interviewer. You have been "looking for work." However, if you give the interviewer that answer, you probably will not get the job. Obviously you are looking for work. The interviewer wants to know what *else* you are doing. Are you

working part-time? doing volunteer work? getting your house in order? having a much-needed rest? All of these answers show that you are an active, thinking person who makes good use of time. Below are some other answers that you might use.

- "I decided I was needed at home."

- "I went back to being a full-time homemaker."

- "I decided to further my education."

- "I was in business for myself."

Whatever your reasons for a job gap, you must assure the interviewer that the condition no longer exists and that you are ready to work. The following statement shows how this is done: "During the past six months I've been self-employed. Now, with the condition of the economy as it is, I find that I need a regular income. I've gotten the desire for self-employment out of my system. I'm ready to work and would like very much to work for your company."

If you have a job gap you need to cover, write your response below.

Employer: "Why do you have this gap in your job history?"

Your response: _____

_____

_____

_____

"What Are Your Future Plans?"   There are several reasons for asking this question. The interviewer may want to know if you are ambitious, if you plan ahead, or if you set goals for yourself. He or she may also want to know what kind of expectations you have of the company. (If you expect too much, you may have morale problems and not stay long.) There are no correct answers. However, you should have a good, positive answer prepared.

"How ambitious are you?" An answer might be "I hope to become very good at my job and perhaps take some schooling to become a top-notch executive secretary." Another could be "I intend to learn the stock so well that I can become a buyer for the department." Both answers tell the interviewer that you want to get ahead and can set realistic goals. They also say that you plan to be around awhile.

Now write your own answer to the question about plans. Emphasize your ambition and use the proof-by-example approach to support your statements.

Employer: "What are your future plans?"

Your response: _____

_____

_____

_____

"What Do You Like to Do in Your Leisure Time?" Interviewers ask this question to see if your activities and hobbies might help the company. (They also want to know if you do more than watch television night after night.) This is your chance to mention community and civic groups to which you belong, hobbies, and volunteer work. If you have held a leadership position in a group, be sure to say so.

Employer: "What do you like to do in your leisure time?"

Your response: _____

_____

_____

The Toughest Questions for You Everyone has a few questions they would rather avoid. In a job interview, however, an employer just might ask those very questions. And if you want the position, you will probably have to answer them. Better to be prepared with a convincing, firm, and positive response than caught off guard.

Think—what are the four questions an employer might ask you that you would have the hardest time answering? If they have not been discussed already, list them below on the numbered rules. Practice your answers by writing them on your own paper. When you have arrived at versions that you feel comfortable with, write your final answers following the questions.

1. Question: _____

Answer: _____

_____

_____

2. Question: _____

Answer: _____

_____

_____

3. Question: _____

Answer: _____

_____

_____

4. Question: _____

Answer: _____

_____

_____

Previewing Basic Interview Questions

The interview questions in the prior section were especially hard ones. You should be prepared to answer many others, however, that are somewhat easier. Below and on the facing page are a large number of such questions. Think of them as simply more tools to help you better prepare for interviews.

Read through the various categories of questions and check off any that might be a problem for you. Then prepare positive answers for them. (If you can't decide which are problem questions, choose those you hope employers don't ask.) When preparing your answers, write them down and save them. Otherwise, you may forget your best responses. Next, practice your answers aloud until they sound and feel right.

When you are satisfied with your answers, do some practice interviews. Look for "interviewers" among your friends and family members. Make each practice interview as real as possible. Pick a certain kind of company for your interviewer to represent. Let your interviewer choose his or her own questions. Use proper manners: start your interviews with a handshake and a greeting. Be sure your answers show that you are dependable and punctual. Also, mention all your relevant skills and interests early on. Try to meet as many employer expectations as possible. And don't let your practice interviewers be too easy on you! Tell them to ask problem questions. They will not help you by being too nice. You cannot count on a real interviewer's being easy with you.

As you practice answering the following questions, use the proof-by-example rating system to score your responses (see page 82). Write your scores on the lines next to the questions. If your scores are low for a particular question, keep working on that response. Also, do extra work on any questions you feel are particularly important for you to answer well.

INTERVIEW QUESTIONS CHECKLIST

General Questions

_____ "What can I do for you today?"
_____ "What is the position for which you are applying?"
_____ "How did you learn about this position?"
_____ "What kind of work interests you?"
_____ "What qualities do you think are necessary to succeed in this kind of work?"
_____ "What do you think might be some of the disadvantages of this kind of work?"
_____ "Why do you want to return to work?"
_____ "What interests you about our product(s)?"

Training Questions

_____ "Do you have any special training?"
_____ "What machines can you operate?"
_____ "Would you prefer on-the-job training or a formal training program?"
_____ "What can you do for this company now?"
_____ "Did you gain any job-related experience while you were in the military?"

Education Questions

_____ "Do you have a high school diploma?"
_____ "What was your rank in your high school class?"
_____ "Why were your grades so poor?"
_____ "Why did you choose your particular major in college?"
_____ "Why did you leave college before graduating?"
_____ "Did you finance part or all of your education? If so, how?"
_____ "What types of books have you read?"
_____ "What were your extracurricular activities?"
_____ "What subject(s) did you enjoy studying most? least?"

Transportation Questions

_____ "Do you have a driver's license?"
_____ "Would you mind moving from this area if the company chooses to relocate you?"
_____ "Can you do considerable traveling?"

INTERVIEW QUESTIONS CHECKLIST (continued)

Availability Questions

_____ "Do you want to work full time?"
_____ "Would you be available for part-time work?"
_____ "What hours would you be available for work?"
_____ "What shift would you prefer?"
_____ "Will you be available for weekend work?"
_____ "Can you work the night shift?"
_____ "Will you be available for overtime work?"
_____ "We rotate shifts every four months. Would this be acceptable to you?"

Work Experience Questions

_____ "What kind of job do you want?"
_____ "What experience do you have that relates to the job you want?"
_____ "What jobs have you held?"
_____ "What did you like most about your last job? What did you like least?"
_____ "How do you know you can do this job?"
_____ "What do you know about this particular position?"
_____ "What do you know about our company?"
_____ "Do you get along well with people?"
_____ "Have you ever had trouble with other people on the job?"
_____ "How would you rate your ability to follow instructions?"
_____ "Can you take criticism without getting upset?"
_____ "What would you do if you had a personality clash with a supervisor?"
_____ "What would you do if you started to become bored with work?"
_____ "What if a personal problem interferes with your performance?"
_____ "Will you fight to get ahead?"
_____ "What have you learned from previous jobs?"
_____ "What do you think determines a person's progress in a good company?"
_____ "What things have you done that show initiative and willingness to work?"
_____ "What supervisory or leadership roles have you held?"
_____ "What qualifications do you have for this job?"
_____ "Why should you be successful in this position?"
_____ "What examples can you give that emphasize your interest in this kind of work?"
_____ "Can you list any examples of your creativity?"
_____ "Are you a good manager? What examples support your claim?"
_____ "Have you ever developed or helped to develop any programs? What kind? How?"
_____ "Have you ever helped to reduce operating costs? How?"
_____ "How would you describe your personality?"
_____ "What do fellow workers think of you?"
_____ "Have you ever hired people before? What do you expect of an employee?"
_____ "Have you ever fired anyone?"
_____ "Can you work well under pressure?"
_____ "Do you like routine work?"
_____ "What was your most important accomplishment during your school years?"
_____ "What did you learn from part-time or summer job experiences?"
_____ "Do you have references?"
_____ "Would your last employer recommend you?"

Future Plans Questions

_____ "What would you like to be doing five years from now? ten years from now?"
_____ "In what geographic location would you prefer to live? Why?"
_____ "How does this position relate to your career goals?"
_____ "How long would you stay with the company if you were offered this job?"
_____ "What other positions have you considered?"
_____ "What is your philosophy of life?"
_____ "Do you plan to go back to school someday?"

Money and Benefits Questions

_____ "What do you expect in terms of benefits?"
_____ "What benefits did you receive from your previous employer?"
_____ "What was your salary for your last job?"

Dealing with Illegal Questions

You should be considered for a position based on your ability to do the job. Unfortunately, not all employers hire on this basis. Some make their decisions for reasons that may not be fair to certain applicants.

To limit such practices, laws have been passed to give all job seekers a fair chance at employment. You've already seen the effects of such laws in the simplified job application forms now being used by so many businesses. In fact, those same laws apply to interviews.

Unless a person has been hired, he or she cannot be asked about race, age, marital status, dependents, health, disabilities, and similar matters. Why? Because such things have nothing to do with one's ability to perform the essential functions of a job. Thus, they are off limits as topics for discussion—either in writing or orally.

Just because it is illegal to ask such questions, however, doesn't mean that such questions don't get asked. They do. Often an employer intends no harm but simply stumbles into a forbidden topic because he or she is a poor or untrained interviewer. The give and take of conversation offers many more opportunities for mistakes than a printed form.

If you are asked such a question, what should you do? You have three options:

- *Point out to the employer that the question is illegal.* No matter how you do this—in a matter-of-fact way, a pleasant way, a humorous way—you are likely to lose a potential job offer. (But you also might be passing on an employer for whom you wouldn't want to work anyway!)

- *Answer the question if it won't hurt your chances for a job.* In many cases, the employer's concern—which may be a legitimate one that has been poorly phrased—will be obvious. Perhaps he or she is concerned that a spouse or children will make a necessary relocation difficult or even impossible. If you are single, then such concerns are less likely to be an issue. Saying so would work in your favor.

- *Answer the concern without answering the question.* Suppose an employer asks, "And how does your spouse feel about moving?" Again, poorly phrased question, legitimate concern, arguably illegal. You can answer, however, without making any reference to marital status: "If you're asking me that question to make sure that I have total freedom to relocate, let me assure you that I do. I thought that matter through very carefully *before* I applied for the job."

The last option is a particularly good solution because it meets the employer's key expectations. The answer is brief, positive, and showcases your transferable and self-management skills. You're thoughtful, organized, and one very good communicator!

Asking Your Own Questions

One of the last interview questions an employer may ask is "Do you have any questions?" The employer asks this as a common courtesy—and as one more test. The job seeker who has no questions will not pass this test. The employer will probably assume that he or she has no serious interest in the position.

You should, therefore, have one or two questions ready. These questions should be assertive, not aggressive. They should show concern for the position and the company. Rather than asking what the company can do for you, they should ask what you can do for the company. But don't waste your questions. Ask for information that really will be useful to you.

The list that follows (at the top of page 93) may serve as a guide to the kind of questions you might ask at the end of an interview. You may use questions from this list or make up your own. Write the questions you want to ask in the appropriate section of your DataTrakt. You may not need to look at them during the interview. However, it's better to do so than to forget or waste an opportunity to gain valuable information.

- "What kind of training might I expect if hired for this position?"
- "Is there anything I can do or study to get a head start on learning this job?"
- "How much supervision would I receive as a new employee?"
- "What hours would I be working if hired?"
- "Will there be a chance to work overtime in this position?"
- "May I see the area where I would be working?"
- "What company is your biggest competitor?"
- "What weakness do you find in my background, relative to this job?"
- "Would you describe your own concept of the ideal employer?"
- "How can I take on more responsibility here?"

Closing the Interview

Seldom will you be offered the position you want at the end of an interview. An employer will generally need some time to consider you as well as other applicants for the position. Indeed, he or she may have other applicants still scheduled for interviews. You may be the best applicant so far. Still, the employer must check other options if the position need not be filled immediately.

Usually an interview will end with the employer's saying, "I'll be contacting you soon to let you know my decision." This should be your cue to begin your callback closing. This closing arranges for you to contact the employer. You might say, "I have several interviews scheduled, but I am very interested in this position. Rather than risk missing your call, when may I call you?" The employer will appreciate this expression of your interest. Also, your callback closing suggests that you should be hired soon—before another employer offers you a job.

Make a mental note of the date and time you are given to call back. (You'll write this data down *after* you leave.) Thank the employer for his or her time. Then present your JIST card. You may say, "Here's the number where I can be contacted if you need to reach me before I call."

This kind of callback closing is simple yet powerful. In the last minute of the interview you will be asserting your interest, your value, and (with your JIST card) your skills, abilities, experience, and other good qualities. Then, when you call back as scheduled, you will be able to show once more that you are reliable and punctual.

Following Up

When the interview is over, don't just go home and wait for the phone to ring. Send a thank-you note—that very same day, if possible. If you are genuinely interested in the job, say so in your note. Enclose another JIST card or at least provide your phone number again. Remember, the interviewer has spent his or her valuable time talking to you. For this alone, the interviewer deserves your thanks.

Handwritten notes are acceptable if your writing is neat and legible. Use good quality notepaper. Consider buying professional-looking thank-you notes at a stationery store in an ivory or off-white color. A clean, typed, professional-looking thank-you note is acceptable in all situations and especially effective in formal situations. Below is a sample thank-you note that should help you write your own.

407 Alcala Road
San Diego, CA 92116
July 30, 1994

Conway Industries
15125 Sylmar Avenue
San Diego, CA 92154

    Attn: Carole Sung
        Office Manager

Dear Ms. Sung:

   Thank you so much for the time you spent with me yesterday. I know you were busy, yet you went out of your way to make me feel relaxed and comfortable during my interview.

   The more I thought about the position we discussed, the more interested I became. I will be in touch with you soon to answer the questions you asked. In the meantime, I just wanted to let you know how much I appreciate the reception you gave me. It's no wonder you have so little turnover in your staff.

Sincerely,

Sally Kijek

Sally Kijek

"Sorry, We Can't Use You Just Now."

When you call back, you may learn that another applicant got the job. You should not be discouraged. The time and effort you put into any interview will not be wasted.

Your interviewing skills will improve each time you put them to the test. You should become aware of weaknesses in your presentation as you use it. You can correct those weaknesses by figuring out how you can better meet an employer's expectations. Remember, practice makes perfect—and actual interviews make perfect practice.

The average job seeker will just quit when the employer calls to say, "Sorry, we can't use you just now." However, you already know that you still have options when told there are no openings. You can use this moment to restate your interest and arrange another phone call, ask about other available positions, or get some job leads.

The Job Offer

The more interviews you have, the more likely it is that you will be offered a job. Most job seekers accept the first offer immediately. However, there are some things you should think about before accepting.

Ask yourself if the separate elements of employment with a particular company seem satisfactory. Consider the position, the company, and the people you would be working with. Also, consider the salary, working conditions, benefits, shift, and duties. All of this information should have come with the job offer. If not, now, after the offer, *is* the time to ask.

Once you have all the information you need, you may indeed accept the job on the spot. You may also want to take some time to think about it. The employer should be willing to give you a reasonable amount of time to consider your decision—24 hours, at least. Finally, you may decline the offer and continue your job search. This isn't as unreasonable as it might at first sound. A job search is not successful just because it leads to a job. The best measure of success is whether or not the job is one you really want and can do well!

7

CHAPTER SEVEN

Finding Job Leads

Uncovering the Hidden Jobs

Through your own dedicated work in this book, you have learned many ways to convince employers of your value to them. This new knowledge will serve you well. Such knowledge alone will not, however, ensure your success. You also need a large number of job leads. The more leads you have, the greater your chances of finding the job you want.

How do you look for job leads? List as many ways as you can think of on the lines below. Try to think of at least five ways. Then circle those methods that you believe will be the most productive.

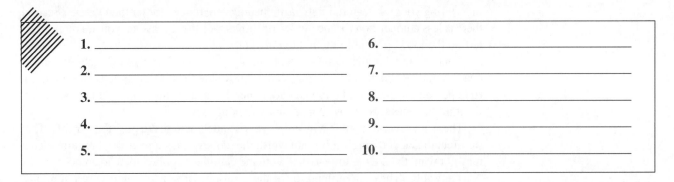

1. _____
2. _____
3. _____
4. _____
5. _____

6. _____
7. _____
8. _____
9. _____
10. _____

Job leads can be either visible or hidden. Visible leads are openings advertised in such places as newspaper want ads and employment agencies. Such leads are easy to find. They are also the leads that most job seekers limit themselves to in a job search.

Hidden job leads are those openings that are never advertised. Because they are not listed in either the newspapers or with employment agencies, it takes some work to uncover them.

There are several reasons why you should not confine your job search to visible leads only, as so many job seekers do. Many of these jobs offer little pay. Others demand special skills, which you are unlikely to have. Visible jobs also create lots of competition because so many job seekers know about them.

The following statements show some of the attitudes job seekers often have after pursuing visible leads. Perhaps you have heard these or similar comments. Perhaps you have even made them yourself.

- "I've been looking for work six months now. What a waste!"

- "The employment office isn't much help. Besides, there are so many other people down there."

- "I read the want ads every day, but there aren't many jobs listed that I'd want. And when I do apply, there's usually a line of people around the block."

These statements show the false belief that very few job openings exist. And this brings us to the main reason why you should not limit your job search to visible openings. *Only 25 percent of all available jobs are ever made visible.*[1] This means that even an active job seeker who depends on visible sources would be aware of only one out of every four job openings!

Jobs do exist. Even in the worst economic times, people retire, move, or quit. For these and other reasons, people are always being hired. In a slow economy, about 1 percent of the work force begins, leaves, or changes jobs each month. In more prosperous economic times, when jobs are easier to find, as many as 2–3 percent of all working people are in a job transition each month. In the United States, this means that there are 1–3 million job openings each month.[2]

This chapter explores methods for finding job leads in both the hidden and the visible job markets. As you read about these methods, compare them with your listing on the previous page. You will probably decide that you can make some big improvements in the way you conduct your job search.

Finding Hidden Job Leads

There are two very good reasons why you should concentrate on the hidden openings during your job search. First, *most* openings are hidden rather than visible. Second, there is less competition for the hidden openings. For these reasons, you are more likely to find the job you want in the hidden market.

Contrary to what the name seems to imply, there are few mysteries about the hidden job market. Each hidden job has an employer with certain expectations about the right person for the job. The job is hidden merely because the employer chooses not to list it in the newspaper or with an employment agency.

There are several reasons why employers decide not to make positions visible. They may feel that advertising a job is not worth the money, time, and effort it requires. They may not want to take the time to deal with the countless applicants who are looking for "just any job." They may intend to fill the position with one of their current employees. Or, they may plan to sort through the applications they already have on file and select the most promising people for interviews. Employers can even wait for the first good job seeker who phones or comes through the front door.

Whatever the employer's reason, you need to solve the mystery of how to find the hidden jobs. Once you do, your job search will be ready for success.

Look at the chart on the facing page. It is based on the largest survey taken of how people actually find jobs. When deciding what job-search techniques to use, it makes sense to choose those that worked well for others. Notice that the two most effective techniques in the chart are applying directly to an employer and asking friends and relatives. Let's look at how you can use these two methods to find hidden job leads.

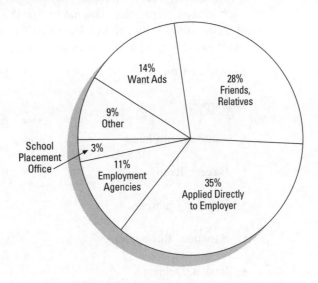

14% Want Ads

28% Friends, Relatives

9% Other

School Placement Office

3%

11% Employment Agencies

35% Applied Directly to Employer

Source: U.S. Department of Labor, Bureau of Labor Statistics, *Job-Seeking Methods Used by American Workers,* Bulletin 1886.

Direct Contact with Employers

The most effective method of finding hidden jobs is to apply directly to employers. Notice in the pie chart you just studied that more than one-third of all people who find jobs find them using this technique.

Most job seekers assume that there must be a job opening before they can obtain an interview with a prospective employer. This is not the case, however. Employers are willing to speak to job seekers even when no job opening exists. Smart employers know that they may need a good employee at some future time. Perhaps someone will quit, business may expand, or someone now on the job may be having problems.

Another factor to consider is that some jobs are hidden from employers! Many employers can create new positions as they see fit. An employer might do this if you prove you have skills needed by the company. So, in this case, the employer sees the right person, then sees the right job. For this reason, you should always be ready for a job lead to become an interview.

The first step in applying directly to employers is to make a list of prospects. This list should include all of the employers who might possibly hire you to do the job you want. Minimal entries should consist of company name, address, and phone number. Further research can provide other useful data, such as the names of the people to whom you should speak.

There are any number of resources you can use to make your lists. Following are brief summaries of the main ones.

The Yellow Pages The Yellow Pages of the phone book make an excellent resource for developing a list of prospects. The Yellow Pages have the most basic, current information about potential employers. In the Yellow Pages, businesses are grouped by the kinds of products and services they provide. This means that you can easily compile a list of companies that might need your special skills. The Yellow Page listings also contain the information you need as a starting point—name, address, and telephone number of each company. Using your basic telephone presentation, you can turn this data into job leads and interviews.

Be complete and creative in your Yellow Pages research. Read all the headings from A to Z. List any that even slightly suggest the job you want. For example, if you wanted a job in food preparation, you might first think only of restaurants. However, looking at the headings in the Yellow Pages, you would see the following groups of jobs that might provide good leads for someone with a background in food preparation.

- Airline Companies

- Airports

- Amusement Places

- Bakers, Retail

- Banquet Caterers

- Banquets, Restaurants

- Basket, Dinners
  see Chicken Dinners

- Beach, Motels
  see Motels & Hotels

- Beach, Resorts
  see Resorts

- Boarding Homes
  see Nursing Homes
  see Rest Homes
  see Sanitariums

- Bowling Alleys

- Buffet Dinners
  see Caterers

Note that only the Yellow Page headings beginning with A and B have been listed. Food service headings from C to Z have yet to be explored. And these are just the categories. Each category includes many potential employers.

Because there are so many potential sources of employment listed in the Yellow Pages, it is important to determine whom you will contact and how. To make the best use of your time, you want to contact first the employers who are most likely to hire you. Therefore, for every category listed in the Yellow Pages, ask yourself, "Could this kind of organization possibly use a person with my skills?" It the answer is yes (or even maybe), list that category.

Some of the categories will sound more interesting to you than others. As you list a category, rate it from 1 (very interesting) to 3 (not interesting at all). Here is an example of how someone looking for a position in food service might organize his or her prospect list from the Yellow Pages.

PROSPECT LIST

Type of Organization	Interest Level
Airline food companies	2
Airport cafeterias	2
Bakers, retail	3
Bakers, wholesale	3
Banquet caterers	1
Banquet restaurants	1
Beach resorts	1

After you have listed and rated the categories in which you might find a job, you need to list individual employers within each category. These are the businesses you will contact. You may want to begin with employers you've rated 3. This will give you an opportunity to improve your phone presentation skills before contacting those employers in whom you are most interested.

Associations and Local Organizations   An association consists of a group of people with a common interest or purpose. Associations differ greatly in their makeup and function. All, however, are potential sources of job leads.

People who do similar kinds of work often form associations. These can be local, state, regional, or national in scope. In the list below, for example, many of the associations are "state/regional" groups. In your area they would be listed under the name of your region, state, or county. Examples would be the Southern California Hotel and Motel Association or the Vermont Retail Council.

- Associated Builders and Contractors

- Association of Plumbing, Heating, and Cooling Contractors

- Federation of Licensed Practical Nurses

- Home Builders Association

- Labor Relations Association

- Mechanical Contractors

- National Motor Carriers

- National Retail Hardware Association

- Society of Broadcast Engineers

- State/Regional Association of Realtors

- State/Regional Electronic Service Association

- State/Regional Food Processors' Association

- State/Regional Hotel and Motel Association

- State/Regional Manufacturer's Association

- State/Regional Restaurant Association

- State/Regional Retail Council

- State/Regional Service Station Dealers Association

- State/Regional Watchmakers Association

Use the phone book to determine what associations are available and of use to you. Research the directory listings Associations, Business Organizations, Trade Organizations, and Labor Organizations.

When you contact an association, ask for a list of all the local businesses employing people to do the type of work you want. Also, ask for any other information that might help you in your job search.

You may want to join associations that you contact. This could help you get some inside information. By attending meetings, you will get to know members of the association. These people may be able to help you in your job search.

Some local organizations are socially or community-oriented. These organizations may help you contact employers. You can find such organizations in the Yellow Pages under Associations/Community, Foundations, and Social-Service Organizations.

The Chamber of Commerce The chamber of commerce is an association. Its purpose is to improve business in a certain community. Your local chamber of commerce can be a good source of information on companies that might need someone with your skills. Many chambers of commerce, especially at the state level, publish directories. These directories contain data on area businesses. Thus, the chamber of commerce is not just a source for job leads. It is also a potential resource for research. Learning such things as a company's size and specialties will help you when an employer asks, "Why do you want to work for us?"

The more you know about a company, the more confident you can be during an interview. However, having just the name of a company that needs someone with your skills is a good start. You can return to the phone book for the basic data you need for a contact.

The Public Library The public library is another valuable resource for hidden job leads. It is overlooked by many job seekers. The library has countless materials to help you in your job search. Just a few of these materials are described below.

- *Telephone Directories.* Many libraries have current phone books for large cities. If you want a job in an area far from your home, these books will be very helpful. Even the local directories can be helpful if you want to avoid distractions at home or you do not have a phone book.

- *Newspapers.* The public library keeps the local newspapers on file. Many libraries also keep major out-of-town newspapers. The library's newspapers can be especially useful when you want to do research to prepare for an interview.

- *Business Directories.* Business directories have the names, addresses, and phone numbers of businesses and their managers. These directories also have other useful data. Some examples of such directories are *Poor's Register of Corporations, Directors, and Executives; The Thomas Register of American Manufacturers; Dun and Bradstreet's Million Dollar Directory; The Federal Register;* and the *Directory of Corporate Affiliations.*

- **Professional and Trade Journals.** Many professions and trades have their own journals and magazines. These publications are concerned with the current trends, history, and the future of their fields. They are outstanding resources. They can help you present an up-to-date, professional image in an interview. These journals may also have information about new markets in the profession or trade. And new markets mean new job leads!

Remember, the resources just mentioned are only a few of the many that you can find at the library. Keep in mind two other factors. First, the librarians can help you find the materials that you need. Second, the service your library provides is free.

Other Resources for Leads to Hidden Jobs

Another helpful resource is the employment contractor specializing in temporary help. This person contracts to do short-term services for businesses, then hires people to do the job. The temporary job can last from one day to one year. This sort of work can help you make some "survival money" so you can continue your job search.

Temporary work can also be a good source of useful information and job leads. If the temporary work is similar to your desired position, you can learn or review procedures and equipment operation. You can also pick up other information that will be important to your future job. Another advantage to temporary work is that you will probably be working with permanent employees. Many of these people can provide job leads. They are likely to know of other places that are involved with similar products or services.

Temporary help agencies hire people for the following types of jobs:

- Accounting/Bookkeeping
- Assembly
- Clerical
- Computer Programming
- Data Processing
- Demonstration
- Factory
- Maintenance
- Marketing
- Project Service
- Secretarial
- Security
- Skilled Labor
- Technical
- Unskilled Labor
- Warehouse
- Word Processing

You can locate temporary agencies specializing in these areas in the Yellow Pages under Employment Contractors—Temporary Help.

Remember, the more job leads you develop in the hidden job market, the sooner you will make direct contact with your next employer. Do not, however, put off contacting employers until you have completed your list of prospects. Your list and your research will probably never be completed! Contact your prospects as soon as you find out about them. You can continue your research for job leads in between contacts and interviews. In fact, you will get many job leads during your quest for interviews. You will learn how to go about making direct contact with employers later in this chapter.

Friends, Relatives, and Acquaintances

Friends, relatives, and acquaintances are often overlooked by job seekers as the important sources of job leads that they are. In fact, they may be your best source of hidden job leads. Recall the pie chart presented at the beginning of the chapter. It showed that 28 percent of all people find their jobs from leads given to them by friends or relatives. Some studies have found that when acquaintances are added to this category, the percentage rises to nearly 40 percent.

All of your friends, relatives, and acquaintances are sources of job leads. These people work in places where jobs open up, and they know other people with job openings. Your goal is to let them know you are looking for a job. They can be especially helpful if they know what sort of job you are looking for and why you are qualified for that kind of work. One effective way to give them this information is to provide them with a JIST card and discuss what you are looking for. Perhaps they know of an opening in your field. If not, ask for the name of someone who might know of one.

Making Your List of Prospects You probably know or have something in common with many more people than you realize. Besides friends and relatives, here are some other groups you might consider:

- Neighbors
- People who attend your church
- People you went to school with
- Former teachers
- Former employers

- People you used to work with
- People you socialize with
- People who provide services to you
- Friends of your parents

To make a list of acquaintance prospects, start with these groups and list any others you can think of. Then develop a list of names from each group. As an example, let's look at the Friends group. We'll say that a friend is anyone with whom you are reasonably friendly and who does not fit into one of the other groups you've listed. If you tried your best, how many names could you think of for this group—10, 25, more? To give you some idea, for all groups, most people can think of well over one hundred names!

Networking A network is a group of people you know who do not necessarily know each other. Any person you know or come to know in your job search can introduce you to others. The illustration below shows how you can begin job-search networks.

How Networks Grow

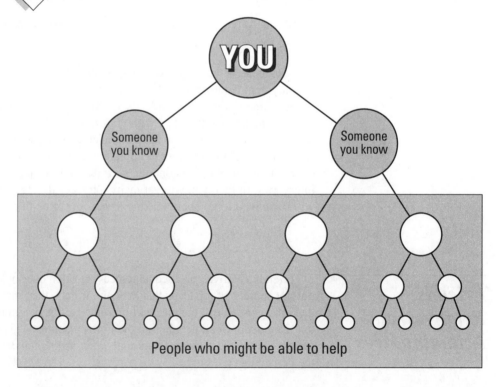

People who might be able to help

Suppose you ask a friend for the names of two people who might help you. You could contact these people, who would then become part of your job-search network. If each of these people gives you the names of two others to contact, and so on, you would eventually have many people in your network. And all from just one original contact!

Do not limit your networking to friends alone. You can start a network with anyone—friend, relative, acquaintance. Work at building up more and more job-search networks as you use all of the different ways to find a job.

Finding Visible Job Leads

The visible job market includes only the jobs that are advertised, posted, or otherwise made available to the public. These jobs make up just 25 percent of all job openings. Newspaper want ads, employment and placement agencies, and government offices are the most common sources of these job leads. Although you may be quite familiar with these traditional sources, you should still carefully review them before using them in your present job search.

Want Ads

About 50 percent of all job seekers use the newspaper want ads as a source of job leads. Unfortunately only about 14 percent of all jobs are obtained through these ads. Still, you should use the want ads. They are the third-leading source of job leads in terms of jobs obtained. The trick is to use want ads as just one part of your job hunt and to use them to your best advantage. To appreciate the advantages of using want ads, you should first review the disadvantages.

Disadvantages Only 25 percent of all job openings are made public. The majority of these jobs appear in the newspaper want ads. This means that you will miss at least 75 percent of all job openings by relying on want ads alone.

Competition can be fierce. When unemployment is high, over 10 percent of the total population looks at the newspaper want ads every week. Half of these people are seriously looking for a job. This means that in a city of a million people, 100,000 are reading the want ads. If the newspaper has 1,000 want ads per day, there is only one job for every 100 job seekers. Of course, the odds are worse for the most desirable jobs. The bottom line is that a job seeker depending only on want ads is competing with anyone who can read!

Some employers use want ads to create or expand their files of potential employees. However, few people are ever hired from these files. A survey of employers in two major U.S. cities showed that 75 to 80 percent of employers do not hire employees through want ads. The other employers hire only 1 out of every 24 applicants who respond to want ads.[3]

In many cases job openings are filled before the want ads appear in the paper. These jobs go to the job seekers who pursue hidden job leads. These job seekers find the jobs while they are still hidden. Job seekers who rely totally on the newspaper do not apply for jobs until the newspaper tells them to.

Tips for Using Want Ads Despite the disadvantages, the newspaper want ads can be helpful. Remember, about 14 percent of all jobs are obtained through want ads. You should limit the amount of time you spend using want ads in your job search. Since only 25 percent of all jobs are advertised, spend 25 percent of your job-search time using them.

The Sunday and Wednesday papers tend to have more want ads than other daily issues. Few employers are available on Sunday. Therefore, you will not lose valuable job-search time if you read the Sunday want ads.

Read the entire Help Wanted section. Sometimes interesting jobs are listed in the least expected place. For example, a secretarial position may be listed under Administrative Assistant or Clerical help. If you look only under *S*, for secretary, you will not see the listing.

Mark all interesting want ads with a pen or highlighter. Then write notes next to the ads if you have any questions or comments. Do this before you respond to the ads.

Pay attention to the type of employers hiring people with your skills. This will help you develop more leads. For example, a baker may find an ad placed by a hospital for a baker's assistant. The baker can assume that other hospitals have openings for bakers from time to time. Hospitals can then be added to the list of prospects.

If possible, research the company and person in charge of hiring before you respond to an ad. However, do not let the ad go unanswered for several days.

Want ads may be in sections other than Help Wanted. Newspapers usually have information about new and expanding businesses. Such information can represent job leads. For this reason you should scan the entire newspaper.

Professional and Trade Journals   If you have a trade or profession, you may obtain publications that deal with your field. These magazines and journals publish information of common interest to people in your field. They also sometimes publish want ads. However, these ads lead to less than 1 percent of all jobs obtained.

Personal Ads   You can place an ad in the Positions Wanted section of a newspaper, trade magazine, or professional journal. This ad should describe the position you want, your skills, and how you may be contacted. However, you must weigh the cost of the ad against the results. Less than 1 percent of all jobs are obtained through these ads.

Employment and Placement Agencies

Most job seekers use an employment agency or placement program in their job search, but only 15 percent actually find a job with this method. The table below shows the percentages of job seekers who have been successful with the various kinds of agencies and programs.

Job-Finding Agencies—How Successful?

Agency	Percent Who Find Jobs
Private employment agencies	5.6%
State employment security division	5.1%
School placement centers	3.0%
Other (unions, miscellaneous)	2.0%

Source: U.S. Department of Labor, Bureau of Labor Statistics, *Job-Seeking Methods Used by American Workers*, Bulletin 1886.

This information shows that these agencies are not nearly as helpful as friends and relatives in obtaining jobs. There are times, however, when using agencies makes sense. Therefore, it is important that you understand what they can and cannot do for you.

Private Employment Agencies   Private employment agencies are in business to make a profit. They charge either the job seeker or the employer, or both, for their services. Some of the problems with using these agencies are listed below.

- Less than 6 percent of all job seekers obtain jobs through private agencies.

- Most agencies depend on a rapid turnover. These agencies do not usually spend much time helping any one job seeker.

- Employers generate most of an agency's repeat business. This means that the agency's emphasis is on helping the employer rather than the job seeker.

- Many agencies concentrate on filling entry-level job openings, which are easy to find. Other agencies specialize in professional and technical openings.

- Only 1 out of every 20 people using a private agency gets a job through the agency. That's a 95 percent failure rate!

- Agencies charge fees of 7–15 percent of the job seeker's first-year pay. This could mean that you would pay well over $1,000 for a job you probably could have found yourself.

In some cases you should consider using a private agency to help you find a job. Those cases are as follows:

- When you yourself cannot spend much time on your job search (when you are employed, for example)

- When you are willing to pay someone else to do something *The Work Book* can teach you to do for yourself

- When you have special, highly desirable, and sought-after job skills

- When you accept only those referrals that include employer-paid fees

State Employment Services The United States Employment Service has programs to help people find jobs in every state. There are no fees for using these services. Most cities and many towns have a state employment office. The offices have different names in different states. (They commonly include the terms *employment security* and *job service*.) For an address, look in the Yellow Pages under the name of your state. These services are often called "unemployment offices" by people who use them.

You should go to the closest state office and register for work. Do not make this your only source of job leads, however. Here's why:

- Only about 5 percent of all job seekers get their jobs through state services.

- In most cases the state offices know of only 5 percent of the available jobs.

- Since over one-third of all job seekers register, competition is fierce.

- For a variety of reasons, many of the placements made by state services are not successful. (Nearly 60 percent of the job seekers leave these jobs within 30 days.)

The best reason to use a state employment service is that it is free. It is also a very good source of training and vocational-testing information.

If you use a state agency, visit the office regularly. Try to see the same counselor each time. To get help, you must be persistent and patient. If you see the same counselor each time, he or she will probably become more and more interested in helping you.

School Placement Centers

Jobs secured through school placement centers represent about 3 percent of all the jobs found. While 3 percent may not sound like much, school placement services have a very high success rate for those fortunate enough to be able to use them.

It would be unwise for you to wait at home for the school placement office to call you for an interview. But you should take advantage of their services whenever possible. Stay in touch with the placement staff, and do anything reasonable that they ask of you. Send them thank-you notes when they provide help. (They probably deserve the thanks and you can always use more friends!)

Government Agencies

Federal, state, provincial, and local governments hire huge numbers of people—as many as one out of every five people hired. For this reason, you should definitely find out what government jobs you might qualify for and how to apply for them. Most phone books have a separate section in the White Pages for government services. Look through this section for the most likely departments. Call them, ask questions, and follow up as required.

You should realize that most government jobs require applicants to take civil service tests or to follow complex application procedures. All of this takes time. While you can often get an appointment to talk directly to the person who can hire you, this person often is forced to hire someone else. Hiring decisions are frequently regulated and based on test scores, application dates, and other factors. If you need a job quickly, do not rely completely on finding government employment.

Other Agencies

There are many agencies other than those mentioned that can help you find a job. Most of these concentrate on helping certain types of people. Most do not charge fees. If you qualify for their services, these agencies can be excellent sources of job leads and other information. Some of the people who qualify for the services of these agencies are as follows.

- *Job seekers under the age of 21.* Some public schools provide classes, job listings, and other help for younger job seekers. Many local, state, and federal youth programs are designed to help young people find jobs. Some of these programs concentrate on summer job placement.

- *Economically disadvantaged.* Many programs are available to people whose family incomes are lower than average. You may not consider yourself poor. However, you may still qualify for these programs.

- *Persons with physical or medical limitations.* Most regions of the country have programs to help people with disabilities find jobs. An example of such a program is the Bureau of Vocational Rehabilitation.

- *Women.* Many organizations have been very active in providing women with job-seeking programs. The YWCA is one example of such an organization.

- *Persons with other special needs.* There are still other programs available for job seekers with special backgrounds or needs. Examples include job seekers over 55 (senior citizens), armed forces veterans, people with criminal records, immigrants, and clergy.

You may qualify for some special services. The Yellow Pages are a good place to start looking for agencies that can help you. If you do not know where to look, ask the telephone operator for assistance. After you find some leads, call the agencies. Ask what they have to offer and whether or not you qualify.

One warning—do not expect any agency to get you a job! An agency may provide you with job leads, but it will also take time away from your own job search.

How to Contact Employers

As soon as you begin to develop lists of potential employers, you should begin to make direct contact with those employers. How do you make direct contact? There are five basic ways:

- Personal referral

- Telephone contact

- Information interview

- Personnel office

- Resume campaign

The first three techniques are recommended for your own job search. The other two are listed because they are common approaches. They are, however, less effective for most job seekers.

Personal Referrals

The most effective technique for contacting employers is to have people the employers know and trust refer you to them. For example, suppose a friend of yours knows an employer who might have an opening in your area. You could contact the employer and introduce yourself as "a friend of John Jones" who, you would say, suggested that you contact the employer. When employers know that you have been referred by a friend of theirs, they are usually very willing to help you. A personal referral is almost always the most effective way to make contact with a potential employer.

Telephone Contacts

The telephone will probably be your most effective tool in direct contact with employers. Chapter 5 describes the whys and hows of using the phone. The telephone is time-efficient and cost-efficient. Even more important, it lets you talk with the employer person-to-person on first contact.

Using your telephone presentation and your list of prospects, call each company or organization in which you are interested. Ask to speak to the person in charge of the job you want. Then get that interview! With this method you will be directly contacting the person who can do you the most good. You will avoid those three or four levels of people who cannot help you very much.

Make as many calls as you can each day. Remember that your goal is to get interviews. If a contact does not result in an interview, ask for more leads.

Using the phone is also an easy way to follow up on want ads and other visible job leads. Just be sure to speak with the person who can hire you.

The Information Interview

The information interview is another method for making direct contact with employers. You can use this method without ever applying for a job. You can also use it to discover hidden job leads and gather valuable information.

To arrange for an information interview, you begin by identifying a few employers who manage jobs like the one you want. You can use any of your resources to locate these employers. Your research should produce the names, addresses, and phone numbers of at least a few businesses.

Next, you should contact an employer. Introduce yourself and explain your interest politely and briefly. Be enthusiastic! Consider the following approach: "Hello, Mr. Tedrow. My name is Katherine Winters. I'm calling you because I'm interested in the local printing and publications trade. I'm considering a future career in the field. I'd be very interested in learning your personal views on it as an industry and as a career. I'd really appreciate it if you could schedule some time with me this week to share some of your insights."

Notice that the caller is honest and forthright about her ultimate purpose—to make a career in the field *if* it proves to be of genuine interest to her. But her primary purpose at this time is simply to gather information. She is not going to put her potential interviewer on the spot to hire her. Such a nonthreatening approach is far more likely to get her a foot in the door than a direct inquiry about existing job openings.

When *does* Katherine ask about a job? Later, after she has thoroughly investigated the field. Then she will be in a position to call back and say that now she knows for sure that she is interested in the company as a potential employer. Of course, by then she'll be a known quantity to the person at the other end of the line. She will have had a chance to impress the employer with her appearance, preparation, work experience (mentioned in passing, of course), and articulateness. In short, while genuinely gathering information, she will have "presold" herself.

Now try following Katherine's lead. In the space below, write your own phone presentation asking for an information interview.

MY REQUEST FOR AN INFORMATION INTERVIEW

_____

_____

_____

_____

Despite this kind of preparation, you should recognize from the start that not all of your requests for information interviews will be received favorably. You should therefore be prepared to conduct a brief interview on the phone. An employer may not be able to meet with you, but he or she may offer to answer a few questions right then and there. If you are prepared, just one minute of an employer's time can mean valuable information for you. It can even result in more job leads.

Meet Employer Expectations   But let's be optimistic. Let's assume you do get an interview. How do you handle it? To conduct a successful information interview, you should be ready, as always, to meet employer expectations. Your appearance should be the same as for a job interview. You should show your dependability by arriving on time. (For this reason, make sure you write accurate notes when arranging the interview.) You can emphasize the third employer expectation—skills—by referring to your skills as you ask questions.

Ask Meaningful Questions   In fact, much of the success of your interview will depend on the kinds of questions you ask. You should plan these carefully. The employer will be more at ease if you are well prepared. Here are some examples of the kinds of questions you might ask.

Information Interview Questions

- "How did you first become interested in this business?"
- "What do you most like/dislike about your profession?"
- "What are the important areas for future development in this industry?"
- "What are some typical daily pressures of managing this sort of business?"
- "What personal qualities are necessary to succeed in this kind of business?"
- "Would you recommend this profession to a person considering it for a career?"
- "What can a person do to get a head start in learning to be a(n)_____?"
- "Would it be possible to arrange a tour of your facilities?"
- "Do you think it reasonable of me to be considering a career in this profession? Besides my sincere interest in this specific area, I . . . (insert a major portion of your complete skills statement)."
- "Do new employees in the (department of the desired position) generally receive on-the-job training or formal training?"
- "Would you agree that (insert your own good qualities from your JIST card) are the qualities of good workers in this trade? What other qualities do you think they should have?"

After you write your questions, pick the 5–10 that you think will produce the most valuable information. You might write these out, leaving enough blank space between questions for notes.

You should take notes during your interview. It is better to do this than to forget something important. Also, your organization and interest may impress the interviewer.

The final questions on your list should be arranged as follows:

11. "I would like to learn more about this business. Can you recommend anyone else for me to contact?"

Name ———————————————— Company ————————————————

Data about person or company ————————————————————

12. "May I use you as a reference when I contact this person?"

——Yes ———— No

These final questions will produce more leads. They will also get you onto another networking level to direct contacts with employers. As you know, if you get the names of two people to contact from an interview, these names can lead to many additional contacts. With these contacts, you will hear about openings before they are listed in the want ads.

Keep It Short and Say, "Thank You" Be sure to leave the interviews after 30–45 minutes unless the employers ask you to stay. At the beginning of the interviews, tell the employers that you know they are busy. Tell them that you appreciate their time and will only stay 30 minutes or so. Do not stay over an hour unless they insist.

Always be sure to thank the employers for their time. It is a good idea to send a thank-you note to each employer a few days later. This note will serve as a courteous reminder of your visit. The note will also supply the employer with your name, address, and phone number. You may include a JIST card with the note. Having this information and knowledge of your interest, an employer may contact you when a job is available.

The Personnel Office

Most people think they should start their job search in a personnel office. However, if you simply walk into a personnel office, you are not likely to talk with the person who can hire you. The personnel staff does not hire anyone. They just screen and refer people for interviews. People on the personnel staff do not know of jobs about to open. They cannot create new jobs for exceptional people like you. This means that unless a job opening is listed, you will probably not be given an application in personnel. Instead, you will hear, "Don't call us; we'll call you."

While personnel office staffs do not hire workers, you can sometimes get help from them. Check to see if any positions you might be interested in are posted. It's always possible. Go out of your way to get to know the personnel staffs at companies in which you are interested. Send these people notes thanking them for the help they've given you. If a job becomes available, they are likely to remember someone such as you who has stayed in touch.

The Resume Campaign

Many job seekers mass mail resumes in the hope that someone will call them for an interview. While this technique does work sometimes, it is far more likely that you will just waste your stamps. One study indicated that a job seeker would need to mail 245 resumes to "To Whom It May Concern" to get one interview.[4] One lesson to be learned from this is that if you do send out an unsolicited resume, be sure to address your cover letter to a person at that company. Do not send your resume to "To Whom It May Concern" or to "Dear Sir or Madam." Better yet, call the person first. If you can't get an interview, then send the resume. And follow up! You'll learn how to prepare your resume in the next chapter.

A Few More Job-Search Tips

Here are just a few more points to keep in mind as you contact employers directly.

Concentrate on Small Businesses Most traditional job-search techniques assume that you are looking for a job with a large business or organization. Yet most people work for small businesses. Small businesses are also a major source of new jobs, and they often offer the best opportunities for learning and advancement. The pay and fringe benefits offered by small businesses frequently do not compare with those offered by larger companies. But a small business could be the place for you if you fit any of these descriptions:

- You are just starting a new career.
- You want more responsibility.
- You are changing careers.
- You need a job quickly.

An additional advantage of small businesses is that they do not have personnel offices. This is good news since it makes the boss easier to contact. Just ask to see him or her. It's often that easy.

Always Follow Up People who follow up get jobs. Send thank-you notes. Arrange to recontact on a regular basis people who appear to be either helpful or potential employers. Consider sending one or more JIST cards and resumes both before and after an interview. Whatever follow-up actions you take will help people remember who you are and what you are looking for. You will also impress them with how well organized you are.

Try Dropping In A very effective way to uncover job leads is simply to "drop in" on employers. You can do this informally, and it is surprising how many people will be willing to see you. This is particularly true of smaller organizations. Be on the lookout for any company that might be able to use a person with your skills. Drop in and ask to see the person in charge. If that person is busy, ask what would be a good time for you to come back.

Using All the Methods

You should now see that all job-search methods have disadvantages. To have the most effective job search, you must use several different methods. And you must use your time wisely. This means spending more time on those methods that have worked well for other job seekers. The worksheet below shows how effective the different methods are.

Worksheet for Job-Search Planning

Technique	Predicted % Success		Total Hours/Week Available		Hours/Week to Use This Technique (rounded)
1. Apply directly to employer	35%	X	34	=	12
2. Ask friends and relatives	28%	X	34	=	9
3. Answer newspaper ads	14%	X	34	=	5
4. Use state employment service	5%	X	34	=	2
5. Send out resumes	5%	X	34	=	1
6. School placement office	3%	X	34	=	1
7. Information interviewing	3%	X	34	=	1
8. Miscellaneous	7%	X	34	=	2

Sixty-five percent of all job seekers spend only 5 hours a week looking for work. If you spend more time, however, you can expect to find a job sooner. You should be willing to spend as many hours looking for a job as you expect to spend working at it once you find it. For example, if you plan to work 40 hours a week, spend 40 hours a week on your job search.

You must also decide how much time you will spend each week using each job-search method. In making your decisions, keep in mind how effective the various methods are.

The job seeker who prepared the worksheet on page 113 plans to use a variety of methods. The job seeker has written a percentage-of-success rate next to each method. From these percentages the job seeker has figured how many hours per week to spend with each method. This job seeker plans to spend 34 hours per week job hunting. Multiplying 34 times the percentage of success gives the number of hours for each method.

Notice that this job seeker plans to spend most of his or her time using the most effective methods. Unless you have a good reason, do not spend more time using a job-search method than its success rate justifies.

Now determine how much time *you* should spend using each job-search method. Read the directions and fill out the worksheet below.

1. Review the methods for obtaining job leads described in this chapter. Then list those that you plan to use at least part of the time. The most effective are already listed on the worksheet since you will probably want to use these.

2. Enter the percentage of success that you estimate for each method.

3. Enter the total number of hours per week that you plan to spend on your job search for each method.

4. For each method, multiply the percentage of success times the total number of hours. This will give you the number of hours per week that you should use that method.

JOB-SEARCH PLANNING WORKSHEET

Technique	Predicted % Success		Total Hours/Week Available		Hours/Week to Use This Technique (rounded)
1) Apply directly to employer	35%	x	_____	=	_____
2) Ask friends and relatives	28%	x	_____	=	_____
3) Answer newspaper ads	14%	x	_____	=	_____
4) _____	_____	x	_____	=	_____
5) _____	_____	x	_____	=	_____
6) _____	_____	x	_____	=	_____
7) _____	_____	x	_____	=	_____

CHAPTER NOTES

[1] United States Department of Labor, Manpower Administration, *Career Thresholds,* Vol. 1, Manpower Research Monograph No. 16.

[2] Richard Lathrop, *Who's Hiring Who* (Berkeley, CA: Ten Speed Press, 1980 revision), p. 19.

[3] Olympus Research Corporation, San Francisco, *Feasibility Study Regarding Classified Ads in Daily Newspapers.*

[4] Deutsch, Shea, & Evans, Inc., *Electronic Design* 16, p. 173.

CHAPTER EIGHT

Resumes
Make Your REZ-oo-MAY Pay

In preparing for your job search, you have learned to make and use various paper tools. Now, after your DataTrakt, applications, and JIST cards, you should consider making your own resume.

A resume does not get you a job. Unfortunately, many people do not realize this. Most often the resume is the only tool they make. They write their resumes, have hundreds printed, and mail them to potential employers. Then they wait for a flood of job offers. Generally they get back only a trickle of responses, and most of these are form letters. Once in a great while, a response contains an invitation for an interview. Seldom is a job offered in response to a resume.

A resume can, however, serve a purpose. It is another tool that can be useful in drawing an employer's attention to you. Like a JIST card, your resume will tell an employer who you are, how to contact you, and the position that you want. It will also describe your experience, skills, and abilities. Unlike a JIST card, however, it will be more detailed and formal.

Your DataTrakt and JIST card will help you make your resume. Refer to them as you work through this chapter.

Perhaps you think that you do not need a resume. Depending on the job you want, this may be true. However, today many employers expect you to have a resume. After completing this chapter, you will be able to satisfy this and other key employer expectations. Here's how.

- *Appearance.* Many employers expect to see your resume during an interview. Like all of your paper tools, your resume will be neat and well organized. This will make a good impression. The effort and care that went into your resume will demonstrate how you will perform on the job.

- *Dependability.* If you have a resume when an employer asks for it, you will be showing that you are dependable. Your resume will also imply your dependability since it will present a totally positive view of who you are and what you have to offer.

- *Skills.* At a minimum, your resume will describe your skills and abilities as well as your work experience, education, and training. Should you choose to spend a little more time on it, your resume could also define and quantify your skills in a way that would emphasize your worth as an employee.

Understanding Various Resume Forms

You can write a resume in either of two basic forms. The most familiar is the chronological form. The other is the functional form. You should understand each form before you decide which is best for you.

The Basic Chronological Resume

The chronological resume form is the one people have traditionally used when making resumes. It lists experiences in order of time. Does this mean that it shows experiences in the order in which they occurred? Yes and no. Notice in the sample below that education is listed before jobs held. This is straight chronological order. You usually get your education before you go out to work. Within each category, however, the entries are listed backwards! College is listed before high school. The most recent job is listed first, the first job last. This is called *reverse* chronological order, and you've seen it before. It's the order required in the Work Experience sections of most job applications.

GENE TAYLOR　　　　　　　　　(317) 555-1492 (home)
123 Main Street　　　　　　　　　　(317) 555-1980 (work)
Littleville, Indiana 46209

EDUCATION:

1986-1990　　Ball State University, Muncie, Indiana
　　　　　　　B.S. in Accounting

1982-1986　　Littleville High School, Littleville, Indiana
　　　　　　　Diploma

EXPERIENCE:

1994-present　Sales Representative, Benko Company,
　　　　　　　Littleville, Indiana

1990-1994:　　Assistant Accountant, Benko Company,
　　　　　　　Littleville, Indiana

1989-1990:　　Student Assistant, Accounting Department,
　　　　　　　School of Business, Ball State University,
　　　　　　　Muncie, Indiana

PERSONAL:

Active in community affairs, willing to relocate.

References available upon request.

Its Good Points The sample resume has a number of pluses. To start, it's brief, clear, and simple. The open, single-page format is easy to take in and read. Even more important, such a resume is quick and easy to prepare. This can mean no time wasted in getting out and calling on potential employers.

In terms of content, the resume's author, Gene Taylor, has been thoughtful and complete. For example, he has provided a number of ways in which he can be contacted. He has given his full address (including zip code) and telephone numbers for both work and home. Thus, he can be reached by either mail or phone. Gene has also indicated that his references are available, but he has not listed them on the resume. Why? This is a courtesy to the people who will provide the references. In this way no one will be bothered needlessly for information. Gene will provide a list of references only after an employer has shown definite interest.

Finally, Gene has taken the time to prepare a good copy. There are no errors in spelling or grammar. He has carefully proofread his resume to ensure that it will make a positive impression.

A First Effort Now try your own hand at a basic chronological resume. Use the form on the next page and insert your own data. When you are finished, make an evaluation. If you think this resume is good enough for your desired job, transfer it to an 8½" x 11" sheet of unlined paper. Keep the major headings—Education, Experience, and Personal—and omit all the others (name, address, degree, etc.).

Use Gene Taylor's resume as a model format. This means that your resume should be typewritten or output from a computer on a laser or laser-quality printer. Read your typed copy carefully. Be sure to check for spelling and grammatical errors. When you're sure your copy is correct, have copies made. You can do this yourself or have it done by a quick-print shop.

The same standards that apply to having JIST cards printed apply to resumes. Remember what you learned in Chapter 4—a white paper tool will blend in with all the others received by employers. To make your resume noticeably different, you should consider using colored paper. You should choose a color that permits easy reading while

still being attractive and businesslike. Some recommended colors are beige, ivory, and pastel shades of yellow, gray, and blue. Recall also that you can project a very professional image by having your resume match or complement the color of your JIST card.

BASIC CHRONOLOGICAL RESUME WORKSHEET

_____   _____
(Name)   (Home Phone)

_____   _____
(Address)   (Message/Work Phone)

_____

Education

_____ – _____   _____
(From)   (To)   (School)

_____   _____
(Degree)   (Location—City, State)

_____ – _____   _____
(From)   (To)   (School)

_____   _____
(Degree)   (Location—City, State)

Experience   (List most recent job first and work backward through your job history.)

_____ – _____   _____
(From)   (To)   (Job Title)

_____
(Company Name)

_____
(Location—City, State)

_____ – _____   _____
(From)   (To)   (Job Title)

_____
(Company Name)

_____
(Location—City, State)

_____ – _____   _____
(From)   (To)   (Job Title)

_____
(Company Name)

_____
(Location—City, State)

Personal

_____

_____

_____

The Improved Chronological Resume

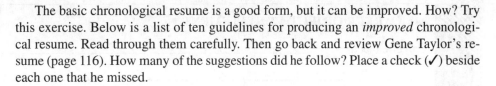

The basic chronological resume is a good form, but it can be improved. How? Try this exercise. Below is a list of ten guidelines for producing an *improved* chronological resume. Read through them carefully. Then go back and review Gene Taylor's resume (page 116). How many of the suggestions did he follow? Place a check (✓) beside each one that he missed.

_____ 1. State a career objective near the beginning of the resume.

_____ 2. Explain specific duties for each position listed.

_____ 3. Detail responsibilities for each position.

_____ 4. Include individual accomplishments for each position.

_____ 5. Make your resume brief but complete, with correct spelling and proper grammar.

_____ 6. Do not leave job gaps in the Experience section.

_____ 7. Make your resume neat.

_____ 8. Do not list salary requirements.

_____ 9. Do not include any negative statements.

_____ 10. Do not list references.

You should have checked the first four items. Gene Taylor could improve his resume by expanding in these areas.

Adding a Career Objective First, Gene should insert a career objective after his name, address, and phone numbers. He has a clear statement of the job he wants on his JIST card. His statement reads, "Position Desired: Sales Representative." This will be the basis for his career objective. He can transfer the statement to his resume by writing, "Career Objective: Position as a sales representative."

Gene can still improve his career objective statement. He should foresee the possibility that an employer might not hire sales representatives. He should be more general and say he wants "a position in sales." Gene should also make his statement in terms that are more vivid. He should use some action words or positive descriptive terms. Employers want active employees who are eager to accept responsibility. He should state his desire for "a challenging position" or "a responsible position." This will set him apart from those applicants who merely want "a position."

Gene can make a final improvement by adding some mention of his skills. His resume shows that he began with the Benko Company as an accountant and later moved into sales. In doing this, Gene learned about both in-house and route sales operations. He can indicate in his career objective statement that he is looking for a position requiring this particular kind of knowledge. His final career objective statement could be "Career Objective: A challenging position in sales. Ideally, this position would require knowledge of and active participation in both inside and outside sales."

It is a fairly simple process to create your own career objective statement:

- Write the title of the position you desire. (Avoid being too specific.)

- Add a word or phrase that implies action or some very positive trait.

- Add a requirement for one or more of your strongest skills.

Now write your complete career objective statement.

Expanding Experience Statements   There are still three elements of Gene Taylor's resume that need improving:

- Explaining the specific duties of each position held

- Detailing the responsibilities of each position

- Including individual accomplishments from each position

These three areas of concern all relate to the Experience section of the resume. It is obvious that more information is needed to improve this section.

By using the sample form below, Gene can organize his information so that he can easily transfer it to his resume. Only one job is shown. Note, however, that a form should be filled out for each position in the Experience section. Notice that Gene has used specific terms of measurement, such as "doubled" and "increased . . . 32%," to show the value of his accomplishments. Think of some similar measures of your accomplishments.

Dates Held: *1994* – *Present*   Position: *Salesman, Benko Co.*

Explanation of Position: *Outside salespeople at Benko are concerned with making direct-to-customer sales in customers' homes.*

Responsibilites of Position: *The promotion of the full line of home-service products made by Benko. Sales in the rural areas of a two-state territory.*

Accomplishments in Position: *Sales in my territory doubled during the years I held the position. I suggested a modification of the accounting system that saved staff time and increased profits by 32%.*

Develop your statements about your duties, responsibilities, and accomplishments in previous positions. Write your statements in the forms provided on page 121. Begin with your present or most recently held position and work backward. If you wish to prepare statements for more than three positions, use the extra forms at the back of the book (page 148).

JOB 1

Dates held: _____ – _____   Position: _____

Explanation of position: _____

_____

Responsibilities of position: _____

_____

_____

Accomplishments of position: _____

_____

_____

JOB 2

Dates held: _____ – _____   Position: _____

Explanation of position: _____

_____

Responsibilities of position: _____

_____

_____

Accomplishments of position: _____

_____

_____

JOB 3

Dates held: _____ – _____   Position: _____

Explanation of position: _____

_____

Responsibilities of position: _____

_____

_____

Accomplishments of position: _____

_____

_____

You should now have a great deal of information to use in improving your resume. Carefully review your information about previous jobs. Pick out those items that present your skills in the most positive way. Then use this information to rewrite your basic resume. The added information will help convince employers that you are more qualified than applicants who have submitted only basic resumes. If you have not had many jobs, include any volunteer, school, or other experiences that show your abilities. Describe the duties, responsibilities, and accomplishments involved in them in detail.

Switching Emphasis By using the information from his form, Gene Taylor wrote an improved version of his original resume. You can see the result below. Gene made one more important change that we haven't yet discussed. He decided that for the job he wanted, his experience was more important than his education. Therefore, he reversed the order of the Experience and Education sections. For the same reason he simplified the Education section. He did this by omitting his high school record and listing only his college degree in accounting. Thus, he included the one feature of his education that would be of most interest to employers.

GENE TAYLOR
123 Main Street
Littleville, Indiana 46209

(317) 555-1492 (home)
(317) 555-1980 (work)

CAREER OBJECTIVE:

A challenging position in sales. Ideally, this position would require knowledge of and active participation in both inside and outside sales.

EXPERIENCE:

1994-present Sales Representative, Benko Company, Littleville, IN

Responsible for direct-to-customer sales in the rural areas of a two-state territory. Promoted 150 home-service products and doubled sales in the territory. Also, suggested a modification of the company's accounting system that resulted in greater sales efficiency and a 32% increase in company profits.

1990-1994: Assistant Accountant, Benko Company, Littleville, IN

Responsible for maintaining an accurate record of the sales activity of Benko's 30 inside sales representatives. Able to revise the handling of records to clarify the sum total of in-house sales activity.

EDUCATION:

1986-1990 Ball State University, Muncie, IN
Bachelor of Science Degree in Accounting

PERSONAL:

Active in community affairs, willing to relocate.

References available upon request.

As you try to improve your own resume, try to select the words that best express your goals and summarize your experiences. The worksheet that follows provides a general format. If you have more data than this form allows, work on a separate sheet of paper.

IMPROVED CHRONOLOGICAL RESUME WORKSHEET

_____   _____
(Name)   (Home Phone)

_____   _____
(Address)   (Message/Work Phone)

_____

Career Objective

_____

_____

Experience

_____ – _____   _____   _____
(From)   (To)   (Position)   (Company)

_____
(Location—City, State)

_____
(Explanation of Position)

_____
(Responsibilities)

_____
(Accomplishments)

_____ – _____   _____   _____
(From)   (To)   (Position)   (Company)

_____
(Location—City, State)

_____
(Explanation of Position)

_____
(Responsibilities)

_____
(Accomplishments)

Education

_____ – _____   _____
(From)   (To)   (School)

_____   _____
(Degree)   (Location—City, State)

_____ – _____   _____
(From)   (To)   (School)

_____   _____
(Degree)   (Location—City, State)

Personal

_____

The Functional Resume

The functional resume focuses on your most important skills. It supports these skills with specific examples of how you have used them. It lets you emphasize those skills that you believe are most important. The functional resume is *not* a chronological listing of your job history. This means that it can help you hide a lack of experience or job gaps. This is the case with the resume shown below. If you are like most people, you'll find its author very impressive. But did he finish college? (Look closely.) How many jobs has he held? For how long and over what period of time? You'll have to wait for the interview to find out!

JOHN H. SHEADY

80 Harrison Avenue
Laurel, California 99643

Home: (303) 379-8276
Messages: (303) 786-6780

JOB OBJECTIVE:

Responsible position in a sales- or service-oriented organization requiring an effective and articulate problem solver.

AREAS OF EXPERTISE:

Communications:
Relate in a friendly, personal style to people of diverse backgrounds. Have considerable experience in formal and informal sales presentations to groups as large as 300 persons. Able to express self clearly in a variety of written formats including complex formal proposals, statistical summaries, correspondence, and promotional pieces.

Sales:
Over a period of years, have consistently demonstrated superior achievement in representing products and services in many different settings. In the competitive food-service industry, "converted" over $1,000,000 revenue annually from competing accounts. Had the highest sales of over 75 people in my division nationally. As an account representative with the Great Widget Company, personally handled sales contracts as large as $150,000. Not simply "order taking," these sales required complex technical analysis, detailed report writing, considerable presales planning, and group presentations. Required extensive travel over a 14-state region.

People Skills:
Have ability to quickly gain trust and confidence. As customer sales representative for a major corporation, accumulated over 80 unsolicited complimentary letters from customers in various positions in supervision and management. Have consistently demonstrated the ability to increase the morale and productivity of people at all levels. Have supervised staffs as large as 15 people.

Problem Solver/Analyzer:
Able to approach large, complex systems and resolve problems to maximize efficiency. In one instance, suggested use of data-processing techniques that resulted in a savings to one customer of over $200,000.

Persistence/Energy:
In virtually all tasks undertaken, have used a natural and spontaneous personal energy to perform beyond expectations. As sales representative, was assigned half the medical facilities in Illinois. During allotted time, visited ALL facilities in area, many of which had not been visited in over three years. Made additional follow-up visits to many of these facilities and *still* remained in the allotted time frame. Results were a 110% increase in annual sales from this region.

EDUCATION:

Northwest Community College -- Computer Science/Math
Argyle Business College -- Business Degree
Independent study -- courses in Sales, Supervision, Management, Customer Service, Public Speaking, and related topics.

PERSONAL:

Married seven years; enjoy challenges; active in community affairs; a participant rather than an observer in life.

REFERENCES AVAILABLE ON REQUEST

To prepare a functional resume you must know what your skills are. You must also know which of these skills you would like to use on your new job. Vocational assessment, career exploration, and interest testing will help you determine the skills that your resume should emphasize. You should also use your DataTrakt, your JIST card, and the employer expectation exercises from Chapters 1 and 2. Then make a list of your skills and examples of how you applied them. When thinking of examples, consider your entire job experience, education, and training.

In the sample form below, Gene Taylor listed one of his skills. He then listed some ways in which he used that skill in previous jobs. Note that job titles, names of employers, and dates of employment are of no concern. The skill, its application, and the resulting accomplishments are the important items.

Skill: _Organization_

How applied (Job 1): _Modification of the accounting system to improve organizational efficiency._

Accomplishment: _Increased profits 32%, increased sales efficiency._

How applied (Job 2): _Revision of record handling._

Accomplishment: _Clarified total in-house sales activity._

Now you try it. In the first blank below write a personal skill that you consider important to the position you want. Then list the specific ways that you have applied this skill and the accomplishments that resulted. If you make a functional resume, use the format above to detail *all* of your skills.

SKILL ANALYSIS

Skill: _____

How applied (Job 1): _____

_____

Accomplishment: _____

_____

How applied (Job 2): _____

_____

Accomplishment: _____

_____

Doing Your Own Resume

Here are some procedures to follow in preparing your own resume.

- *Ask a friend or vocational counselor to read the first draft of your resume.* Ask for suggestions on how to improve it.

- *Always use language that is action-oriented and positive.* You want "a challenging position." You are an "experienced" worker. You "have dealt" with a number of specific tasks. Also, try to keep your sentences short. (You may even want to use phrases.) And illustrate your points with specific examples. Taken together, all of these techniques will help make your writing striking and memorable.

- *Make sure that everything in your resume relates to the position you want.* Do not waste even one second of an employer's time with unrelated details.

- *Do not list a specific job title.* This will limit the possible uses of your resume.

- *Do not spend so much time writing your resume that you delay your job search.* If you follow the guidelines in this chapter, you should be able to complete a well-organized resume fairly soon. After using your resume awhile, you will know which parts, if any, need improvement.

- *If possible, have your resume output by a computer hooked up to a laser or laser-quality printer.* Another, more expensive alternative would be to have it typeset and printed on good-quality paper.

- *Try to get your entire resume on one side of one sheet of paper (8½" x 11").* An employer is more likely to read the entire resume if it appears to be short.

All of these suggestions are fairly straightforward. One that might require some additional explanation, however, is the second, about language. What kind of language is "striking and memorable"? You could probably use some examples. Study the list of useful words and phrases that begins below.

Useful Words and Phrases

It is important to use action words and positive descriptions in a resume. Employers want to know what you accomplished in previous jobs, school, and volunteer work. This is no time to be shy!

Look through the following list of words and phrases. Check off those that fit you and apply to your desired job. See if you can use these and similar words in your resume.

About You and Your Strengths

_____ assertive	_____ enthusiastic	_____ trustworthy	_____ manager
_____ bilingual	_____ motivated	_____ achiever	_____ motivator
_____ competent	_____ organized	_____ administrator	_____ problem solver
_____ cooperative	_____ punctual	_____ coordinator	_____ risk taker
_____ dedicated	_____ reliable	_____ developer	_____ specialist
_____ dynamic	_____ responsible	_____ fast learner	_____ trainer
_____ effective	_____ skilled	_____ generalist	_____ troubleshooter
_____ efficient	_____ talented	_____ leader	_____ willing worker

About Your Skills and Abilities

_____ analyze	_____ establish	_____ modify	_____ write
_____ assist	_____ priorities	_____ plan	_____ work well
_____ communicate	_____ implement	_____ practice	with others
_____ compose	_____ increase	_____ recruit	_____ work well
_____ conceive	productivity	_____ schedule	under pressure
_____ create	_____ increase profits	_____ solve problems	_____ understand
_____ delegate	_____ initiate	_____ supervise	
_____ develop	_____ innovate	_____ teach	
_____ economize	_____ interview	_____ train	

Preparing Cover Letters

You should *always* include a cover letter when you mail your resumes to potential employers. The cover letter is the first thing an employer should see and read. It introduces your resume.

Your cover letter should be brief and interesting to ensure that your resume will be read. Here are some rules to follow in preparing a cover letter:

- *Always send your cover letter to someone in particular.* Do not sent it to anyone in a personnel department unless you know the name of the person who supervises the position you want. Be certain that you have all names, titles, departments, and other details spelled correctly.

- *Make your letter neat and error-free.* As with your resume, appearance counts. One error or one case of poor physical appearance will create a lasting negative impression with that particular employer.

- *Target your letter to the situation.* A few typical reasons for sending a cover letter and resume include preparing an employer for your interview (the best reason), responding to an ad, and following up a phone call after you have promised to send information. Each situation requires a different approach. Take advantage of the opportunity to provide special information that is not on your resume but which may be of particular interest to the employer.

- *Be clear about what you want.* If you want an interview, ask for it. If you are very interested in the particular organization or position, say so, and then tell why you think you would do a good job. An informal and friendly, but professional, style that avoids the hard sell usually works best.

- *Plan to follow up.* Do not expect someone to contact you. Instead, mention that you will contact the person at a specific time unless an interview or some other activity is already set.

On the facing page are sample cover letters that have been written for some common job-search situations. Use these samples to build on as you develop your own letters.

Using Your Resume

Your resume is a highly detailed paper tool. You will want to use it often in your job search. Some of its uses are similar to those described for your JIST card. For example, after filling out an application, attach your resume with a paper clip or staple. If you do this, potential employers are more likely to see you the way you want them to see you.

As Information for References and Network Members

You may want to give copies of your resume to your references. The resumes will help these people write and speak positively about you. Your resume will also give them information about the position you want.

Why is it important that your references have this information? References are people who have favorable opinions of you and your abilities. However, they may know you only from one situation, such as work, school, or church. With a copy of your resume in hand, each person will be aware of your other experiences. This added information will help them highlight your history. In particular, they will be able to discuss how your experience and qualifications suit you for the job you are seeking. Your resume will also help remind former employers exactly when you were employed and what your position was.

You should also give copies of your resume to family members and friends whom you have asked to "be on the lookout" for potential jobs. Your resume will remind them of the kind of position you want. When the opportunity comes up, your "lookout" can give a resume to a potential employer.

As an Interest Builder

Mail your resume to potential employers. However, do not mass mail your resumes randomly. Remember, if you mail 245 resumes randomly, you can expect to receive just one request for an interview. You will be far more successful if you use your resumes to follow up specific leads. After promising telephone contacts, you can mail resumes to those certain employers. Perhaps a telephone contact almost but not quite got you an interview. A follow-up resume and another phone call might do the trick.

As a Follow-Up Device

After an interview you may leave your resume with the interviewer as a "super" business card. Thank the interviewer for his or her time and arrange for a follow-up call. Later, when you phone, your resume will remind the employer who you are and what you have to offer. It will also tell the interviewer how to contact you.

628 Holly Road
Starlight, Pennsylvania 15339
February 29, 1995

Ms. Mary Klasky, Director of Operations
Short Optical Corporation
2020 Vision Way
Starlight, Pennsylvania 15339

Dear Ms. Klasky:

When our mutual friend, Jane Logan, suggested that I call you, I had little hope of getting through to you so quickly. Thanks so much for setting up an appointment to see me so soon.

I have been interested in the vision business for some time now, and I believe I am ready to make my contribution to this field. Just seeing firsthand how an efficiently managed and growing organization works will be a worthwhile experience for me.

I have enclosed my resume for your information. I will be at your office promptly at 9 a.m. next Thursday, March 5.

Sincerely,

Debbie Tamashiro

Debbie Tamashiro

5413 Harrison Avenue
South Bend, Florida 41267
September 5, 1994

Mr. Paul Hernandez
The Travel Store
1900 Avenue of the Americas
New York, New York 10052

Dear Mr. Hernandez:

As promised, I have enclosed a copy of my resume. Please look it over within the next few days. Perhaps you will think of a few people whom I can contact.

Your suggestions for breaking into the travel business in New York have already been helpful. I called Ms. Karl right after I spoke with you, and she has agreed to see me during my trip to New York. Thank you for the lead. She made me promise to say hello when I spoke with you next.

Based on the good reception I have received, I have now made firm plans to be in New York during the last week in October. I would like to see you if at all possible during that week. I will call you soon to arrange a meeting.

Thanks again for all of your support in my job search. Please call me at home if you hear of anyone who is looking for a bright and ambitious travel agent.

Sincerely,

Fred Marsik

Fred Marsik

21 W. Rayen
Stevensville, Kansas 62348
March 23, 1994

Mr. Bob Arnold, Personnel Director
Anonymous Corporation
223 Placer Drive
Stevensville, Kansas 62347

Dear Mr. Arnold:

I read with interest your ad for a secretary in the *Stevensville Times*. As requested, I have enclosed my resume for your review. Since I am certain that you will receive many resumes, let me give you a few reasons why you should sort mine into the "I want to interview this person" pile.

I have selected the secretarial field as my career. For me, it is not just a way to earn a living. As proof of this, I have taken a variety of secretarial courses throughout high school and have completed the Professional Secretarial Program at the Stevensville Business Institute. This is a one-year, full-time program with course work in accounting, office management, word processing, and other advanced topics. Besides receiving a B+ average in this tough and demanding program, I held a full-time job at the same time.

In addition to my training, I have had a variety of work and life experiences that have helped me understand more than most people my age. For example, I have learned to work quickly with large numbers of customers in a busy restaurant environment. The sensitivity to people's needs and ability to solve problems quickly are as useful in an office as they are in other work settings.

Being dependable is also one of my virtues. I have not missed a day of school or work, for example, during this past year. In fact, I like to work. I like being with people, staying busy, and doing assignments well.

Since you will probably need to make a decision on this soon, I will give you a call this Friday morning, March 28, to provide answers to any questions you may have. While I will be busy with my job search during most weekdays, you can leave a message for me at any time on my answering machine. I will return your call at the earliest opportunity.

Sincerely,

Mark Saraj

Mark Saraj

CHAPTER NINE

Organizing Your Job Search

Ready, Set, Go!

You now know a great deal about job hunting—much more than most of your competitors. Knowing something, however, is not the same as being good at it. As you have learned throughout this book, being good at job hunting requires practice. And the best way to get job-hunting practice is to go out and do it!

Spend as much time as possible on your job search. Remember, even if you spend only 25 hours, you will be spending many more hours than most other job seekers.

As you begin to use some of the methods you have learned, you may feel uncomfortable, shy, and afraid of making mistakes. This is natural. You will sometimes be aware of what you could have done better. In school, work, and life, this process is called *learning*. Do not let this fear of making mistakes keep you from going on. Understand that one interview is just one of many you will have. There will be bad ones as well as good ones. There will be rude employers just as there are rude people in all other positions. The trick is to learn from every experience you have during your search. Improve those things that can be improved—and keep on going!

This chapter contains samples of some schedules and forms that will help you in your job search. These paper tools include the following:

- *Daily job-search plan.* This schedule outlines the necessary daily activities in the life of a job seeker.

- *Daily/weekly and monthly job-search planning calendars.* These forms serve as an "appointment book" during a job search. They remind you when and where your interviews are.

- *Networking and direct contact forms.* These forms are based on several job-search ideas presented in Chapter 7.

- *Follow-up cards.* These are 3" x 5" cards designed to remind you of the details of each contact and how you should follow up.

Do remember in using these forms and schedules that your objectives should be fairly simple:

- Commit at least 25 hours per week to your job search.

- Arrange two interviews per day.

- Do your best in interviews.

- Follow up.

If you do these things, you will get a job faster than if you do not. It is that simple.

Using a Daily Job-Search Plan

It's easy to *say* spend 25 hours on a task. It's harder to envision *how* to spend that much time on it. To help you out, this part of the chapter provides a sample daily plan (see below). This schedule tells you when to do various kinds of job-search activities and how. It also lists the materials you will need to carry them out.

Sample Job-Search Plan

- **8:00 A.M.—Get Ready!**
  1. Equipment you will need:
     a. Clean desk or table at which to work (preferably in a quiet place where there are few distractions)
     b. Telephone (one you can use without a lot of interruptions)
     c. *The Work Book* (as a reference to keep your job-search skills sharp)
     d. Newspaper want ads, the Yellow Pages, and other sources of new job leads
     e. Pencils and pens, envelopes, stamps, 3" x 5" cards
  2. Forms you will need:
     a. Completed telephone-contact script
     b. JIST cards
     c. Resumes (if you need them for your search)
  3. Anything else you think you might need.

- **8:30 A.M.—Gather New Leads!**
  1. Get at least 15 new job leads from all sources:
     a. Check your networking lists for any friends, relatives, or acquaintances you haven't contacted yet.
     b. Check your direct contacts list for other types of organizations you could contact.
     c. Check other sources such as want ads and employment agencies for job leads.
  2. For each new lead, prepare a follow-up contact card *before* you make any calls.

- **9:15 A.M.—Check Old Leads!**
  Check old follow-up cards, planning calendars, and other sources for people you can call back today.

- **9:45 A.M.—Take a Break!**

- **10:00 A.M.—Make Telephone Contacts!**
  1. Have these things (and only these things) in front of you:
     a. Telephone
     b. Telephone-contact script (to read from until you have it memorized)

    c. Follow-up cards for new leads

    d. Follow-up cards for old leads

    e. Planning calendar (to record new appointments for interviews and other activities)

    f. Pencils and pens, 3" x 5" cards, and notepad (if needed)

2. Begin making your calls:

    a. Call all new leads.

    b. Make callbacks and do other follow-ups.

    c. Do not make a new call until after you have recorded the results of your previous call on your follow-up cards and planning calendars.

    d. Send thank-you notes, resumes, or JIST cards as necessary for any calls you make.

    e. Plan to make enough calls (20–30) to get two interviews a day.

- **11:30 A.M.—Wrap It Up!**

1. How many telephone contacts did you make today?

    a. Total your calls to new leads.

    b. Total your callbacks.

    c. Total all other types of calls you made.

2. How many interviews did you get today?

    a. Be sure you have clearly written the company name, address, date, time, and interviewer.

    b. Verify this information has been inserted on your planning calendar(s).

3. How many applications, JIST cards, and resumes do you need to drop off, fill out, or mail?

    a. Be sure you have clearly written company names, addresses, dates and/or times promised, and contact names.

    b. Verify this information has been inserted on your planning calendar(s).

4. What do you have lined up for tomorrow?

    a. Total new callbacks scheduled, new leads from friends and relatives, etc.

    b. Verify this information has been transferred to follow-up cards.

- **12:00 NOON—Pat Yourself on the Back and Go to Lunch!**

- **1:00 P.M.—Begin Your Active Job Search!**

1. Go to your interview appointments.

2. Keep appointments to fill out applications and to drop off JIST cards and resumes.

3. Try to set up interviews at the companies you visit.

4. If you don't have appointments, consider these alternatives:

    a. Visit companies for whom you would like to work and try to set up interviews.

    b. Set up information interviews with "hard-to-crack" companies.

    c. Check in with any agencies or offices helping you with your job search.

    d. Check in with your vocational or job placement counselor, if you have one.

    e. Get more leads and make more phone calls.

    f. Work on thank-you notes for interviews you have had.

    g. Complete any other work important to your job-search.

- **5:00 P.M.—You're Done for the Day! Good Job!**

By now it should be obvious—looking for a job is hard work. So, when you've finished, reward yourself. Make a point of relaxing with friends or family. Take the time to do something you enjoy.

Even on your off time, however, you can let people know that you are looking for a job. Everyone is a possible contact for you and can become part of your network. You can also use evening and weekend time to read or review job-search materials, work on improving your resume, contact your working relatives, or do other job-search activities.

Now try working up a daily plan of your own. Use the sample you've just read as a framework, or modify it to suit your own needs.

Preparing Your Own Job-Search Schedule

In Chapter 7 you decided on the number of hours per week you planned to spend looking for a job. Now you need to break that number of hours into a daily schedule. Start with this worksheet.

Scheduling Worksheet

Days	Number of Hours	Time Periods
Monday	_____	_____ to _____
Tuesday	_____	_____ to _____
Wednesday	_____	_____ to _____
Thursday	_____	_____ to _____
Friday	_____	_____ to _____
Saturday	_____	_____ to _____
Sunday	_____	_____ to _____

Then ask yourself the following questions, and insert your answers on the worksheet in the appropriate columns.

- *Which days of the week do you want to spend looking for a job?* Circle those days on the worksheet.

- *How many hours will you spend looking for a job on each of these days?* Write your answers in the second column of the worksheet, right next to the days you circled. (Be honest with yourself. Write a number, or numbers, you can stick to.)

- *What time periods during these days do you want to spend looking for a job?* In the third column of the worksheet, write in the times you will be conducting your job search. For example, you might want to observe a standard 9–5 workday.

When you've finished, you will have the framework of your own job-search schedule. You will be ready to enter those days and times into calendars that will allow you to do both long-term and short-term planning of your job search.

You do your long-term planning on a monthly calendar form like the one shown opposite, at the top of the page. (You can either make your own or buy a tablet of blank calendar forms.) You begin by entering your selected times on the appropriate days for each week. You do this at least four weeks in advance. Why? Because planning your schedule that far in advance will prevent you from scheduling less important events during these times.

You do your short-term planning on a daily/weekly calendar like the one shown opposite, at the bottom of the page. Once again, you can make your own form or use one

Monthly Job-Search Calendar   APRIL 1994

Sunday	Monday	Tuesday	Wednesday	Thursday	Friday	Saturday
					1 Job Search 9-12 -Call Smith/ Silver Lake Bakery	2
3	4	5 Job Search 9-5	6 Job Search 9-5 Hines -Info Interview (2pm) Brenda's Place (dessert/pastry chef) Brenda Cucci (3:30pm)	7 Job Search 9-5	8 9-12 Kitchen/Cookware Show - Convention Ctr. (1-4)	10
10	11	12 9-5 Miller's Interview (baker's asst.) Harvey Wrightman (3:30pm)	13 9-5	14 9-5 Jonathan's Inn Info Interview Sdra Muntz (3pm)	15 9-12 Mountains →	16
17 (Mountains)	18	19 9-5	20 9-5	21 9-5	22 9-12	23
24	25	26 9-5	27 9-5	28 9-5	29 9-12 Mountains →	30

Daily/Weekly Job-Search Calendar

	Sunday 4/3	Monday 4/4	Tuesday 4/5	Wednesday 4/6	Thursday 4/7	Friday 4/8	Saturday 4/9
9:00			Finish	Follow ups-	Follow up	Weekly	
9:30			cafeteria list	old leads: Rilling's	Hines leads	Wrap-up	
10:00			Call cafeterias	Sherm's Mkt Mr. Myers etc.	↓		
10:30			↓	↓			
11:00					Make contact cards		
11:30			↓	↓	Thank-you notes-		
12:00			Make contact cards	Update contact cards	Hines & Cucci	Irene -	
12:30			LUNCH	LUNCH	LUNCH	LUNCH+	
1:00			↓	↓	↓	Kitchen/	
1:30			Bakery visits-			Cookware Show -	
2:00			Spath's (res.)	Mary Hines- Info Interview	(Begin cafeteria visits?)	Convention Ctr.	
2:30			Chez Nous (JIST)		↓	↓	
3:00			Daily Bread "				
3:30				Brenda's Place Brenda Cucci			
4:00				(pastry chef position)		↓	

that is preprinted. Do one daily/weekly calendar for each week of your search. As you make appointments for interviews and other activities, enter the place and kind of appointment. List this information in the appropriate time slot under the correct day.

You should list some of this information on your monthly calendar as well. Use the monthly calendar to schedule the active job-search time you plan. Also, list any interviews you schedule or future reminders.

In planning your daily routine, consider organizing your time into four-hour blocks. This is similar to a typical eight-hour workday. Work from 8 a.m. to noon gathering leads and making telephone contacts. After lunch, work from 1 p.m. to 5 p.m. keeping interview appointments, visiting companies, and doing other activities. (The sample job-search plan presented earlier in the chapter conformed to this pattern.)

A daily schedule, not one but two different kinds of calendars—you may be asking yourself, "Why go to all this trouble?" Think again. If you follow a routine similar to that described in the sample job-search plan, you will be extremely busy. You will be juggling dozens of names, dates, times, addresses, phone numbers, forms, conversations, interviews, and inquiries. Your calendars will be very important in keeping you organized.

Keeping Track of Your Contacts

In Chapter 7 you learned how to develop networks of people who can help you develop job leads. You also learned how to develop leads for making direct contact with employers. As your networks and lists of direct contacts grow, you will need to carefully organize and keep track of your leads.

One organizational tool you will need is a networking form. You will use this form to list the people and organizations you plan to contact for one day. Create a simple form of your own using the entries and headings shown here.

Networking Form

Name	Organization/Referral	Follow-Up Prepared?	Comments
1. Mary Hines	Friend of John Pass	yes	Knows people
2. Fred Farkel	Friend	yes	Following up
3. Spoth's Bakery			I shop there
4. Silver Lake Bakery	Want ad	yes	Baker's position
5. Miller's Grocery	Want ad	yes	Baked Goods Department
6. Uncle Paul's Chinese Eatery	Listed in magazine	yes	Irish/Chinese Food
7.			

A direct-contact list is another simple form you can make for yourself. You will use this form to list the companies and organizations within the Yellow Page categories described in Chapter 7. Since you will not usually have much information about these contacts, you will postpone preparing a follow-up card until after you have finished the call.

Direct-Contact List

Category: _Cafeterias_

Name of Organization	Address	Phone Number
1. Albert C. Smith's Eatery	8614 N. Central Avenue	782-5699
2. Alfonso's Cafeteria	29 North Way	467-2211
3. Brenda's Place	Southway Drive	779-8257
4. Fritz Farkel's	4513 Armstrong Drive	329-4068
5. Jonathan's Inn	Johnson Street	526-7782
6. Lisa's French Foods	86 Central Avenue	669-4415
7.		

Following Up

If you follow the suggestions in this book, you can develop hundreds of contacts to use in your job search. You will not be able to keep track of all of these leads unless you keep notes and develop a way to organize your information.

Below you will find an example of a completed follow-up card that you can make yourself using 3" x 5" cards. Prepare one card for each person or organization that you may want to follow up with later.

Follow-Up Card

Organization: _Silver Lake Bakery_

Contact Person: _John Smith_   Phone: _421-9987_

Source of Lead: _William Henry – former supervisor_

Notes: _Called 3/29/94. Mr. Smith is on business trip; will be back 4/1/94. Call then._

Get an inexpensive file box with tabbed dividers for your cards. You will need one divider for each day of the month. When you want to follow up with someone on, say, the 15th of the month, put that follow-up card behind the 15th. When that date comes up, you will know exactly whom to contact.

Good Luck!

Good luck with your job search. Job hunting is often discouraging, and it can be one of the most difficult jobs you ever have.

Take care of yourself, and don't give up. If necessary, accept a "survival" job while you continue to look for the job you really want.

You now know the most effective job-search techniques. It's up to you to use them. Luck will play a part, but remember—the harder you work, the luckier you are likely to be.

APPENDIX

......

Duplicate Forms

JOB-RELATED SKILLS

Skill statement: _____

_____

Example: _____

_____

_____

_____

Connection: _____

_____

_____

JOB-RELATED SKILLS

Skill statement: _____

_____

Example: _____

_____

_____

_____

Connection: _____

_____

_____

JOB-RELATED SKILLS

Skill statement: _____

_____

Example: _____

_____

_____

_____

Connection: _____

_____

_____

TRANSFERABLE SKILLS

Skill statement: _____

_____

Example: _____

_____

_____

_____

Connection: _____

_____

_____

TRANSFERABLE SKILLS

Skill statement: _____

_____

Example: _____

_____

_____

_____

Connection: _____

_____

_____

TRANSFERABLE SKILLS

Skill statement: _____

_____

Example: _____

_____

_____

_____

Connection: _____

_____

_____

SELF-MANAGEMENT SKILLS

Skill statement: _____

_____

Example: _____

_____

_____

_____

Connection: _____

_____

_____

SELF-MANAGEMENT SKILLS

Skill statement: _____

_____

Example: _____

_____

_____

_____

Connection: _____

_____

_____

SELF-MANAGEMENT SKILLS

Skill statement: _____

_____

Example: _____

_____

_____

_____

Connection: _____

_____

_____

MY WORK EXPERIENCE STATEMENT

_____
_____
_____
_____
_____
_____
_____
_____

MY WORK EXPERIENCE STATEMENT

_____
_____
_____
_____
_____
_____
_____
_____

MY EDUCATION AND TRAINING STATEMENT

_____
_____
_____
_____
_____
_____
_____
_____

MY EDUCATION AND TRAINING STATEMENT

_____
_____
_____
_____
_____
_____
_____
_____
_____

INTERESTS AND HOBBIES

Statement: _____
_____
_____
_____
_____

Connection: _____
_____
_____
_____

INTERESTS AND HOBBIES

Statement: _____
_____
_____
_____
_____

Connection: _____
_____
_____
_____

PRACTICE JIST CARD

(Name) _____   (Home Phone) _____

_____ (Message Phone)

(LEAVE SPACE)

(Target Heading) _____   (Job Objective)

(LEAVE SPACE)

(Value Heading) _____   (Experience Statement) _____

_____

_____

_____

(Education Statement) _____

_____

_____

(Job-Related Skills Statement) _____

_____

_____

(Transferable Skills Statement) _____

_____

_____

(LEAVE SPACE)

(Problem-Solving Statement) _____

_____

_____

(LEAVE SPACE)

(Self-Management Skills Statement) _____

_____

_____

PRACTICE JIST CARD

_____   _____
(Name)   (Home Phone)

                                                  _____
                                                  (Message Phone)

(LEAVE SPACE)

_____   _____
(Target Heading)   (Job Objective)

(LEAVE SPACE)

_____   _____
(Value Heading)   (Experience Statement)

                                       _____

                                       _____

                                       _____
                                       (Education Statement)

                                       _____

                                       _____

                                       _____
                                       (Job-Related Skills Statement)

                                       _____

                                       _____

                                       _____
                                       (Transferable Skills Statement)

                                       _____

                                       _____

(LEAVE SPACE)

_____
(Problem-Solving Statement)

_____

_____

(LEAVE SPACE)

_____
(Self-Management Skills Statement)

_____

_____

BASIC CHRONOLOGICAL RESUME WORKSHEET

_____   _____
(Name)   (Home Phone)

_____   _____
(Address)   (Message/Work Phone)

_____

Education

_____ – _____   _____
(From)   (To)   (School)

_____   _____
(Degree)   (Location—City, State)

_____ – _____   _____
(From)   (To)   (School)

_____   _____
(Degree)   (Location—City, State)

Experience   (List most recent job first and work backward through your job history.)

_____ – _____   _____
(From)   (To)   (Job Title)

_____
(Company Name)

_____
(Location—City, State)

_____ – _____   _____
(From)   (To)   (Job Title)

_____
(Company Name)

_____
(Location—City, State)

_____ – _____   _____
(From)   (To)   (Job Title)

_____
(Company Name)

_____
(Location—City, State)

Personal

_____

_____

_____

_____

_____

_____

JOB 1

Dates held: _____ – _____   Position: _____

Explanation of position: _____

_____

Responsibilities of position: _____

_____

_____

Accomplishments of position: _____

_____

_____

JOB 2

Dates held: _____ – _____   Position: _____

Explanation of position: _____

_____

Responsibilities of position: _____

_____

_____

Accomplishments of position: _____

_____

_____

JOB 3

Dates held: _____ – _____   Position: _____

Explanation of position: _____

_____

Responsibilities of position: _____

_____

_____

Accomplishments of position: _____

_____

_____

IMPROVED CHRONOLOGICAL RESUME WORKSHEET

_____   _____
(Name)   (Home Phone)

_____   _____
(Address)   (Message/Work Phone)

_____

Career Objective

_____

_____

Experience

_____ – _____   _____   _____
(From)   (To)   (Position)   (Company)

_____
(Location—City, State)

_____
(Explanation of Position)

_____
(Responsibilities)

_____
(Accomplishments)

_____ – _____   _____   _____
(From)   (To)   (Position)   (Company)

_____
(Location—City, State)

_____
(Explanation of Position)

_____
(Responsibilities)

_____
(Accomplishments)

Education

_____ – _____   _____
(From)   (To)   (School)

_____   _____
(Degree)   (Location—City, State)

_____ – _____   _____
(From)   (To)   (School)

_____   _____
(Degree)   (Location—City, State)

Personal

_____

SKILL ANALYSIS

Skill: _____

How applied (Job 1): _____

_____

Accomplishment: _____

_____

How applied (Job 2): _____

_____

Accomplishment: _____

_____

How applied (Job 3): _____

_____

Accomplishment: _____

_____

SKILL ANALYSIS

Skill: _____

How applied (Job 1): _____

_____

Accomplishment: _____

_____

How applied (Job 2): _____

_____

Accomplishment: _____

_____

How applied (Job 3): _____

_____

Accomplishment: _____

_____